following jesus &
leading people

The stories in this book that serve as examples and illustrations of contemporary Christian leadership are all adapted from real events. The names have been changed to protect the people involved. In a few cases it was necessary to change other details, as well as names, to preserve anonymity. However these stories represent real people, situations and dynamics.

Scripture Union books are published in Australia by:
Scripture Union Resources for Ministry Unit
Locked Bag 2
Central Coast Business Centre
NSW 2252
www.scriptureunion.org.au

and in the United Kingdom by:
Scripture Union
207-209 Queensway,
Bletchley, MK2 2EB, England
www.scriptureunion.org.uk

The National Library of Australia Cataloguing-in-Publication entry

Farley, Ross.

Following Jesus, leading people.

ISBN 1 876794 39 9.

1. Leadership - Religious aspects - Christianity. 1. Title.

253.53

Cover and text design by RokatDesign.com.au, Australia.
Printed and bound in Australia by Openbook Print, Adelaide 1060-04

perspectives on

following jesus & leading people

biblical ways of being
an influence for Jesus

Ross Farley

Scripture Union

Dedicated to
Lyn

contents

Foreword
7
Acknowledgments
11

Introduction
13

1. No Looking Back
15

2. Change-focused Leadership
33

3. People-centred Leadership
57

4. Valued-based Leadership
79

5. Team-empowering Leadership
101

6. Looking Forward
119

foreword

I was recently invited by a young friend to come and hear him preach his first sermon. The church was a fair distance from my home, and had been running 'youth' services for quite some time. It is a phenomena occurring in literally hundreds of places every week across this country.

I arrived, took my seat and then scanned the assembled group, numbering about thirty, mostly aged between 16 and 30, with a sprinkling of grey heads. The service was full of subdued passion, with singing and praise, and prayer and preaching. But my mind started to think: 'What would Jesus do with this group, and all their intentions and passions? How does this group of young Christians become a world transforming presence?'

Nearly 2000 years ago, Jesus gathered such a group. They couldn't have been much older than my young friends in that church, and they came with all the impetuosity, passion, pessimisms and unpredictability likely in any group of young people. Yet Jesus shaped, moulded and sent them out, under the guidance of The Holy Spirit, to change the world.

Shaping leaders was a primary work of Jesus earthly ministry. We need only read John 17 to understand that Jesus was intentionally developing his followers for an important ongoing work. The Gospels speak about Jesus working, shaping his disciples with a clear missional intent to proclaim the Reign of God across the whole world, in word and action, raising up others who would do likewise. Shaping leaders was, and is, core to this work, the most important in all eternity.

That's why I am pleased to endorse and recommend Ross' book. Ross understands the challenge of producing leaders for God's purposes, and has been on the cutting edge of producing young Christian leaders for many years. Scripture Union is indebted to Ross for his vision in founding and directing the Youth Ministry Internship Scheme, a 'hands on' practical training program for youth workers, pastors, chaplains and mission workers.

Many young men and women across Australia will have cause to thank God for Ross, for his patient, tough and dedicated work in their lives, helping them to hear and respond to the call of Jesus to stand up and be counted, and then shaping their capacity and skills for effective Christian leadership.

This book represents some of the most important lessons Ross has learnt, lessons that he teaches and embodies. In a world period where leaders are constantly exposed for poor ethics, self interest, domination and rationalism, Ross points us back to stories of Jesus working to build leaders with character.

In a world where leadership theory has become a complex science, to be approached by only the most qualified, Ross reminds us that leadership is, at its core, influence.

Students will find this book extremely helpful in building paradigms and skills within themselves, as will coaches and mentors working with emerging leaders.

Those who have been leaders on the road for a while now, will find this work a helpful corrective to the character drift that so often wrecks Christian leaders.

But most valuable of all. Ross exposes a well kept secret. Leadership is not an elite pursuit. Anyone can become a better leader. Jesus' example calls and leads us all to be people of character and influence.

So, get off that couch, awaken that passion, tap that potential, learn from Jesus the Master, and watch God develop the leader within you.

David Tolputt
National Director
Scripture Union Australia
July 2004

acknowledgements

The research that formed the basis of this book, was initially done for a Master of Arts thesis in the *Faculty of Arts and Sciences of Australian Catholic University*. The thesis was entitled *Jesus and Contemporary Leadership Theory*. This book is a very different piece of literature, but the work done in that thesis was an important stepping stone to the writing of this book. With that in mind I would like to express my thanks to Brian Kelty, my supervisor during the writing of the thesis, who helped me to think through many of the issues that are explored in this book. I would also like to thank another lecturer, Francis Moloney. I have acknowledged him a number of times in the text of this book, but his help in linking the leadership of Jesus as recorded in the gospels, to contemporary practice, was far more pervasive than those acknowledgements suggest.

Thanks also should go to those who helped me compile the contemporary examples and illustrations, all drawn from real events. Obviously these people must remain anonymous, but their assistance in collecting and recording these stories is significant. There are also numerous friends and colleagues I would like to thank for discussing these issues with me and helping me clarify my thoughts. They know who they are.

Ross Farley

introduction

In many ways this book is a reflection of my own struggle to understand leadership. I have pondered the nature of leadership for decades and my quest can be summarised with two questions:

What is leadership?

People have given me answers to that question since I was a teenager, however, I was never really satisfied with their explanations. For example, I was told by some that the leader is the person in charge, so leadership is what that person does. It didn't take me long to work out that it was often the people who were not in charge who had the most influence. Other explanations about the nature of leadership were equally unsatisfactory.

I think I have begun to understand leadership and I hope that this book will help you to understand leadership more clearly too. Leadership is one of those things, where understanding what is going on, makes a huge difference.

How does the practice of Christian leadership today, fit with the example of Jesus?

My concerns about a lot of contemporary Christian leadership are a result of reading the Bible. If I did not read the stories of Jesus, I don't think I would have asked the questions that led to the writing of this book. Frankly, in many areas, I see huge gaps between the example of Jesus and the leadership practices of Christians today. Yet we are supposed to be the followers of Jesus.

Read on, if you want to explore these two questions.

no looking back

no looking back

What can we learn about leadership from the example of Jesus?

How would our practice of Christian leadership change if we took Jesus as our starting point?

These questions and others like them are explored in these pages. As we examine Christian leadership, we take Jesus' example of leadership as the one we should follow. We assume that those who claim to be Christian leaders, should, first and foremost, be followers of Jesus.

This book does not examine the whole life of Jesus, drawing material from here and there to discover how Jesus led. It would be possible to construct a body of teaching about the leadership of Jesus by selectively putting together some of the things he said, some characteristics he displayed and ways he interacted with people and situations. Such an approach could possibly produce some valuable insights but there is a danger that it could be quite skewed and misleading. In contrast, rather than selecting material from a broad sweep of the gospels, this book examines, in detail, a number of specific gospel stories and analyses the leadership issues involved.

Stories about Jesus' leadership

Why have I chosen to examine the leadership of Jesus through gospel stories? I think leadership is best understood in the context of actual events. In the gospel stories we see Jesus facing situations and engaging with people. This is how leadership actually happens. By understanding the stories, we can begin to understand the dynamics involved in the leadership of Jesus. Leadership is not about possessing a set of character traits or occupying positions of authority. Leadership is about relationships between leaders and followers who are in specific contexts and face particular issues. This interplay between characters, relationships, contexts and issues comes to life in the gospel stories.

The four stories I have chosen to explore are the call of Simon, Andrew, James and John (Mark 1:14-20), the call of Peter (Luke 5:1-11), the call of Levi or Matthew (Mark 2:13-17) and the appointing of the twelve apostles (Mark 3:13-19). I chose these four stories because they come at the beginning of Jesus' relationship with his disciples. (If we are going to understand the relationship between Jesus and his disciples, it is best to start at the beginning.) Another reason is that these particular four stories provide good examples of four major themes of leadership. That is, leadership should be change-focused, people-centred, value-based and team-empowering. As such, these stories provide the basis for a balanced examination of leadership issues. Of course, there are many stories about Jesus that have not been examined in this book. If they were to be explored, other issues and principles would emerge as well as the ones identified in this book.

I want to make it clear that I do not believe that the gospel writers wrote these stories about Jesus to teach us about leadership. It is very likely that the gospel writers may not have been aware of some of these leadership issues when they wrote these stories. In some cases, I may be observing in an ancient text, concepts that were quite foreign to the original readers. So, at the beginning of each chapter I attempt to provide some interpretation of the story before observing some leadership issues in each story.

Preliminary comments about leadership

It is important to realise that leadership is a twentieth-century concept. This book does not have the space for a discussion on the emergence of leadership as a concept. Joseph Rost extensively researched both the concept of leadership and the use of the word leadership and arrived at the following conclusions.[1]

> Leadership did not come into popular usage until the turn of the century, and even then lacked the connotations people attach to the word today. Those connotations seem to have begun to take shape in the 1930s, but they did not have a great impact on scholars and practitioners until after World War II...

> ...Leadership, as we know it, is a twentieth-century concept, and to trace our understanding of it to previous eras of Western civilization (much less other civilizations) is as wrong as to suggest that people of earlier civilizations knew what, for instance, computerisation meant.

To say that leadership is a modern concept does not mean that people in ancient times had no idea about anything to do with leadership. They understood that shepherds led sheep, kings ruled countries and military officers commanded soldiers. However these ideas fall far short of modern concepts of leadership. The development of the social sciences in recent centuries has provided the intellectual tools to conceive, and begin to articulate, a concept of leadership. In the ancient world, political leadership was seen as a possession, exclusively owned by kings and handed down to their firstborn sons. Uprisings aside, ordinary people simply had no say. Political leadership in modern democracies is a totally different concept. The masses choose whom they will follow.

This does not mean that leadership did not happen in ancient times. Gravity happened before Isaac Newton discovered it, but people had no concept of gravity. Before Newton, people took for granted that items fell to the ground and stayed there. Similarly, two thousand years ago, Jesus provided an example of leadership and many people chose freely to follow him, but those people would not have understood his activity in terms of leadership. People called him rabbi, teacher, master, Messiah, Christ or Lord. They did not speak of Jesus as leader. When we think of the leadership of Jesus, we are trying to understand the ancient story of Jesus according to modern concepts.

Leadership is a very misunderstood concept. This may well be because, as a concept, it is still relatively new. Sometimes leadership is confused with being the best in a particular field. Often people who are very skilful are exercising leadership, but this is not necessarily the case. Some of the tensions that exist with people in leadership can result from simply not understanding what is going on. When people develop a better understanding of leadership, expectations become more realistic and some of the difficulties disappear. Part of the purpose of this book is to clarify the nature of leadership.

Leadership happens on many levels. One misconception of leadership is that it is only the pastor of the church, the head of the organisation, the chairman of the board who exercises leadership. In Chapter 2, I argue that leadership is not confined to particular organisational positions and can happen at any level of a church or organisation. Leadership even happens in informal groups of friends, when it is usually not even thought of as leadership. While this book has important principles for pastors and heads of organisations, it also has much to say to anyone who wants to influence people for Jesus.

Throughout this book I refer to, or quote, numerous sources. Some of these are New Testament scholars who have helped me to understand the Bible text. Others are leadership scholars, many of whom have written texts that are used in universities. I don't necessarily agree with everything they have written but I have found many of their insights very helpful. Most importantly, I have tried to identify the ones that are consistent with the leadership practices and principles of Jesus.

Stories about contemporary leaders

Many Christian leaders are very Christ-like in the way they exercise leadership. Yet sadly, there are also numerous examples of 'Christian leadership' that seem to be completely at odds with the practices and values of Jesus. The following stories demonstrate how bad things can get when Christian leaders lose sight of Jesus. Some of the characters in these stories demonstrate very positive examples of leadership, yet all three stories have examples of leadership that completely contrast to Jesus' way of doing things.

Michael's story

I first met Michael when I was the guest speaker at an interdenominational youth camp. Young people had come from numerous churches, but the four young people who came with Michael were from very different backgrounds from most of the others. At first, they didn't mix with the other campers, staying outside during the meetings and generally inhabiting the fringes. They seemed like spectators looking in on the camp rather than campers. Michael explained to me that the four of them had only recently become Christians. When he had first met them they were part of a group of about a dozen street kids and drug addicts. Michael had become their friend, encouraged them to get off drugs, supported them through the difficult withdrawal process and helped them to improve their lifestyle. Michael had also explained the gospel and all four had decided to become followers of Jesus. They were now having regular Bible studies and were eagerly growing in their faith. Michael had brought them to this particular camp so that they could meet some other Christian young people. They found it very difficult to mix with all the other young people at first, but, as the camp progressed, they gained confidence and began to mix freely. Towards the end of the weekend, they even shared their stories with the rest of the camp.

Michael had done a great job with those four young people and had exercised a kind of leadership that reflected the values of Jesus. The interesting thing is that he was not a youth worker, but a middle-aged family man, the senior pastor of his church. If anything, he seemed a little on the conservative side, not at all the sort of person you would expect to find working with street kids. He didn't usually have anything to do with teenagers at risk, but had met these 'by chance' and things had developed from there. It was not long though, before other leadership emerged in his church, in opposition.

A few months after camp, Michael phoned me. When I asked how the young people were going on, he told me that they had started coming to church. However, Michael had been confronted by an influential person in the church who said that he, and a number of others in the church, did not feel comfortable with those particular young people around. The young people in question hadn't caused any trouble at the church. During the time they had attended the church, nothing was stolen or broken, and Michael had even left them alone in his home. Despite this they were shunned by most of the church people, and treated as a source of constant amusement. Michael was told not to waste his time on people like them, an instruction which caused considerable conflict for him. He reluctantly tried to explain to the young people the poor attitudes that they had encountered in the church and then encouraged them to attend another church where they were more likely to be warmly welcomed. Months passed before I received another phone call from Michael. He told me that virtually all of the young people of his church had left, including those who came from church families and the children of the church elders. The church members thought that this was a terrible state of affairs and that something had to be done. Michael phoned to ask me if I would be willing to meet with the church and help them work out what to do.

Some weeks later a meeting was held and anyone who was concerned about the youth of the church was invited to attend. The church elders were in attendance as well as a good number of others. I started by asking, 'What would you like the youth ministry of this church to achieve?' The overwhelming response could be summed up as 'entertainment'. If the entertainment was good enough, they believed the young people would come to church and the problem would be solved. I explained that although there is value in entertainment other things might also be important. That's when things got really interesting.

I said that churches often have young people, who are keen to follow Jesus and would like some Bible input and other activities to help them grow in their faith, as well as entertainment. I was quick to add that I realised that although many young people are not ready for that, it is important to consider the needs of those who are serious about discipleship, as well as the uncommitted. At this point a few men began to dominate the discussion. They were adamant that the teaching of the Bible would be counter productive, even if there were some young people who were keen. They were insistent that entertainment was all that was needed for young people to come, even though the church's existing model of youth ministry was entirely entertainment based, and the young people had still left. In the past, Michael had led a youth group that had more of a discipleship focus, but some in the church with influence had forced it to be closed.

It was time to change tack, so I suggested that, when they ran youth programs to entertain their youth, they could also invite young people who don't go to church, so their programs could also serve as outreach for unchurched young people in the community, and address their spiritual, social or physical needs. At this point, one of the elders stood up and said, 'You don't get it, do you, Ross? The problem is not that other young people will not come to church. We don't care about anybody else in our community. The only problem is that *our* teenagers don't come to church. We brought you here to tell us how to get our young people to come back to church. We don't care about reaching our community - the only thing that matters is whether our young people come to church.'

These were not the sentiments of people on the fringes of the church, but the attitudes of the leadership, those who made the decisions in the church. Michael told me later that there were people in the church who really did care about reaching their community, but they were not the ones who carried the weight. The most concerning aspect of the whole experience was that the opinion leaders of that church did not seem to have the slightest awareness of how much their values, attitudes and behaviour were so diametrically opposite to the example of Jesus. It was not long after this meeting that Michael decided to seek another ministry position.

'No looking back!' That's a common expression that affirms the need to be whole-hearted and single-minded. Jesus employed similar imagery when he said, *'No one who puts his hand to the plough and looks back is fit for the kingdom of God'* [2]. Yet there is a sense in which we should look back. We should look back in time to Jesus, our example of leadership. Paul wrote, *'Follow my example, as I follow the example of Christ'* [3]. Paul looked back to Jesus, and then moved forward with the example of Jesus in mind. I would like to suggest that one of the problems we face in contemporary Christian leadership is that we don't look back to Jesus enough.

Michael's story contains a blatant example of Christian leadership that completely contrasts with the leadership of Jesus. In many churches and groups such attitudes may never be put into words, but they are, nevertheless, the attitudes that call the tune. Could you imagine Jesus turning away the group of young people in the story above? Would he think that helping them was a waste of time, particularly when they had responded so positively? Do you think he would oppose teaching the Scripture? Would he attempt to reach people beyond the community of faith?

Deborah's story

In the previous story, it was the lay leadership that drove many of the problems. In this one, a professional leader is involved. Deborah's story is about how she endured, and finally escaped, a very manipulative pastor. Unfortunately, some Christian leaders do not seem to appreciate that leadership is quite different from control and manipulation.

Deborah originally moved to her new church with great enthusiasm and encouragement from Neil, the senior pastor. She was immediately placed in the position of music director (her area of training) and flourished in this role, taking on a part-time position and developing the music team to one of the strongest ministries in the church. Deborah's employment in the church extended to full-time and she also accepted various administrative roles. As the years progressed, she recognised that a pattern was occurring which stemmed directly from Neil's leadership style.

A group of individuals would continually fill higher positions of leadership in the church, like a vortex with the pastor in the middle, but as soon as anyone got too close, they were repelled. Those who left the church were generally labelled 'not a child of the work' and departed in conflict and shame. Members of the church were often emotionally abused for contacting those who had left. Neil's daughter ignored one of Deborah's friends for months for talking with Deborah after her departure. Such things happened time and time again, and each time Neil would highlight some hideous sin that had caused the person to leave. In Deborah's case, she was a 'Jezebel spirit', who never really had a heart for the work. He would also spread rumours of a personal tragedy, claiming that these were God's punishments on those who had abandoned the work. These scenarios were generally lies or, at least, extreme exaggerations. Deborah's first-born child had a minor birth defect that was corrected within a few weeks. Neil insinuated to people that her baby had massive deformities, as a result of God's judgement.

People in positions of leadership all left for similar sorts of reasons. Often it was frustration over a leadership style that revolved around Neil's whims, such as cancelling Deborah's music team meetings with no consultation. There was also concern about a leader who demanded extreme loyalty, to the extent of making the church their family, above their own families. For example, Neil rebuked Deborah for informing her parents of her pregnancy before him. Then there was alarm because of the very loose accountability around finances. Neil refused to hold Annual General Meetings. He also dissolved a finance committee after the first meeting, because questions were raised about the high salary he had set for himself. Others left because of distress caused when Neil disadvantaged people to benefit his own family. Deborah was asked to continue in her role voluntarily due to lack of finances, but within a few months Neil's daughter filled another paid position in the church. Almost every one, who got too close, left for these sorts of reasons. The only people who remained in paid positions in that church, after Deborah left, were members of Neil's family

– each with a church paid vehicle and multiple real estate assets, purchased through income from the church.

Deborah endured seven years of being told that she was not spiritual enough, not pastoral enough, not 'led by the Spirit', not worth her pay. She finally left a few weeks after being told, fifteen minutes prior to a general leadership meeting, that her position as music director was to be filled by one of Neil's sons, and she was to work under him. This was the final straw.

Most will readily see the problems in Neil's leadership behaviour. His treatment of people went unchallenged because he claimed that he was called and appointed by God, and therefore his behaviour must not be questioned. He gave the impression that God judged people who did not comply with Neil's wishes, reinforcing that by spreading misinformation about those who disagreed. Continuing members didn't learn the truth because he prohibited contact with people who had left.

The disciples of Jesus were called and appointed by the Son of God himself. Could you imagine Jesus teaching them to behave as Neil did? There are many stories like Deborah's story. The details of these stories vary, but they boil down to one thing: Christian leaders who believe that they can do whatever they like, because they see themselves as above criticism and exempt from accountability.

There will always be moral lapses among leaders, but this book is not primarily concerned with the moral and ethical failures of leaders. Religious leaders have been having affairs and abusing their positions since before the time of King David. These moral lapses are significant problems, but they are usually seen as failures. Neil probably believed that his leadership behaviour is the way that Christian leadership should be done. Unfortunately, it falls far short of the teaching and example of Jesus.

Mark's story

Consider a different leadership situation. Mark is the senior pastor of a growing church, well respected by the vast majority of his congregation. He is supported by the associate pastors, but opposed by Doug, a very influential member in his denomination. Mark's congregation is growing at a healthy rate of over 7% per year and it has a very high conversion rate of 8% per year. That is, for every 100 members, an average of eight unchurched people become Christians, are baptised and join the church every year. As far as conversion rates are concerned, Mark's church is consistently one of the top performers in the state, for his denomination.

Mark and his church follow a ministry philosophy of grass roots evangelism and discipleship. They make it a priority to cooperate with other churches and groups in their community and deliberately avoid strategies that would attract people to leave other churches to join their church. The priority is the growth of the kingdom of God in their district and what happens in their church is part of that broader picture. They are involved in a host of community activities, from ministry in schools to efforts to help the homeless. The church is also a big financial supporter of both local and overseas mission and in the last twelve months has massively increased its giving to these ministries.

Despite all this Doug thinks Mark is unfit to be a senior pastor. On one occasion, Doug visited Mark in an attempt to persuade him to resign. He told Mark that he believed the congregation would never ask him to leave because of their respect for him. Doug then demanded that Mark resign because he was not a leader and was inhibiting the growth of the church. Doug's case against Mark boils down to three points. Firstly, Doug believes that there is only one valid style of leadership and that is the Chief Executive Officer (CEO) style. Doug wants Mark to adopt this style, which is often employed in the world of business. Mark does not disagree with the CEO style as such but agrees it might be suitable for some people and some contexts. The problem is Doug's insistence on the CEO style being the *only* valid style and his stance that anyone not complying with that style, is not fit to lead.

Secondly, according to Doug, the only measure of a church is the number of people who attend the Sunday morning service. He believes a pastor with a congregation of 1000 is ten times more successful than a pastor with 100, regardless of whether these people have transferred from another church or have been converted. According to Doug's philosophy, it does not matter how much personal growth these people experience; the number of people who attend is the sole measure of success. In some ways this is quite consistent with the approach of business, from which the CEO model originates. Businesses exist to produce or sell products and the more the better. The difficulty in Christian ministry revolves around such questions as, What is the product? and How do you measure it? For Doug the answer is clear. All he wants is a large crowd of people in the Sunday morning service, even if he has to steal them from other churches or cut back on other ministries in the community. Mark is not opposed to large churches and his own church has a congregation of a reasonable size. The problem is that in Doug's eyes, the number attending the Sunday morning service is the only valid way to evaluate a church. Ministry in the community simply does not rate.

Doug's approach would also mean that Mark would have to change his attitude to the other churches in his community. Mark had always seen the other churches as fellow workers in a shared mission. Doug was insisting that, from now on, Mark view the other churches as competitors. In Doug's view, Mark could never be a successful leader until he launched an effective and deliberate campaign to sheep-steal from the other churches in the district. Other Christians in the community should be seen as competitors, not brothers and sisters in Christ. He wants Mark to view his church as a business that must maximise its market share.

Thirdly, according to Doug, the only way to be a good leader is to have a big congregation, and the only way to have a big congregation is to have a big building. Doug had proposed that Mark's church build a large building in place of their current one. This would require taking out a massive debt and redirecting their giving from mission to infrastructure for years to come. The congregation rejected this proposal and that was when Doug turned against Mark.

How might a congregation pay for a large building? The answer is to attract people from other churches. The more the attendance at the Sunday morning services increases, the more money is collected and the easier debts can be repaid. That is why Doug views attendance at the Sunday morning service as the sole indicator of the success of a church, because that is where the collection is taken. Community ministry costs money, while Sunday services make money.

All this requires a consumer approach to worship in which people are entertained to keep them coming to the Sunday morning service. Mark has no problem with the services being entertaining, but Doug insists that Mark should only tell people what they want to hear. Doug has rebuked Mark for preaching on social or moral issues. It seems that Doug believes that preachers should never call for repentance, because that is not what people want to hear and that services must entertain and uplift people, not challenge them.

Compare Doug's approach to that of Jesus. Underlying all of Doug's approach is the idea that there is only one way to be a leader. John the Baptist's leadership style was different from the way Jesus led, yet Jesus did not criticise John for doing things differently. Later Paul's leadership followed Christ-like principles, yet the way he applied those principles, was sometimes quite different from Jesus. New Testament churches probably operated in a variety of different ways. It is very difficult to argue from the Bible that there is only one way to be a leader.

It is hard to imagine Jesus using the attendance at Sunday morning services as the sole measure of a ministry. He certainly attracted large crowds at times, but he also placed a priority on training his disciples, healing and casting out demons. Community needs and discipleship seemed to be considered more important than big crowds. Jesus never built a church building and the early church did without buildings for centuries, *and* grew much faster than the contemporary Western church. I have no objection to church buildings as such, but the example of Jesus is markedly different from that of people like Doug, who make buildings a very important pillar of their leadership philosophy.

Could you imagine Jesus, the Lord of the church, wanting his people to compete with other local churches and deliberately try to steal their members? It is worth noting that Jesus (and his disciples) continued to participate in the corporate worship of Judaism all through his life, by attending the temple and worshipping in the synagogues. It was not until after the resurrection of Jesus that the Christians separated from Judaism.

Doug's philosophy about money would be very difficult to harmonise with the teaching and example of Jesus. As for preaching, Jesus did not worry if the message turned people away. He told enquirers to count the cost and deliberately put his finger on the issues that people needed to face. It is hard to imagine that Jesus was telling the rich young man or the Pharisees what they wanted to hear. If Doug applied his leadership criteria to Jesus, he would have to conclude that Jesus was a hopeless leader. Jesus completely contradicts every one of Doug's criteria for a good leader. Now I don't believe that Doug is deliberately trying to disobey Jesus. He is, no doubt, a sincere Christian who is committed to the Lord Jesus Christ and wants to serve him. The problem is not that Doug has rejected the Bible. The problem is that Doug has learnt his model of leadership from the world of business and is imposing it on churches, without even stopping to evaluate it against the teaching of the Bible and the example of Jesus. Doug is only aware of one way to do leadership and he is probably totally unaware that his model contradicts much of what the Bible teaches. Christian leaders can learn a lot from business, but we should not unthinkingly copy business practices without critiquing them against Jesus and the Bible.

Endless leadership stories

The three examples above shows how contemporary Christian leadership can fall short of the example of Jesus. These stories all involve people who would claim to be evangelicals, have a high view of the Bible and most likely believe that they are doing leadership the proper way. They would simply be unaware of the huge gap between their leadership practice and that of Jesus. In each story, different issues can be identified where contemporary practice contrasts with Jesus. We could collect endless stories like these from current practice and compare them with Jesus but in this book I plan to take the opposite approach. I will take four stories about Jesus and try to discover what they teach us about leadership today. My presupposition is that Jesus is the Christian's most important model of leadership. Obviously there are some ways in which we can't be like Jesus, but there are many ways in which we can. Where we can, we should follow his example. So we will start from Jesus and having looked at his leadership, try to apply his example to contemporary Christian leadership.

Deeper issues

While this book is about leadership, there are four deeper questions that lie beneath the surface of the discussion.

1. How should Bible stories be applied to today? Just because Jesus did something, do we have to do it today? If we take it to extremes, we would only ever wear sandals, because that is what Jesus wore. This is a difficult issue, but there are principles in Jesus' ministry that ought to be embraced by Christian leaders today.

2. What should be the relationship, between knowledge gained from the social sciences, and that gained from the Bible? Christians believe that the Bible is the inspired Word of God, the touchstone for life and doctrine, yet we can also learn from the social sciences. How do we find our way between the Bible and the social sciences? Some Christians take a 'nothing but the Bible' approach and try to ignore the social sciences. Most of these people are probably not aware that they are influenced by the social sciences. Even when they prepare children's talks, they very likely utilise insights from modern education. At the other extreme there are Christians who are so open to every idea, that they embrace anything that comes their way. They rarely stop and ask what the Bible has to say, and they may end up adopting practices that are quite contrary to the teaching and example of Jesus. I believe that we ought to learn from the social sciences as well as from reflecting on ministry practice. However we should always critique our practices against the Bible and particularly the example of Jesus.

3. What does the Bible have to say about ministry processes? As evangelical Christians, we readily accept that the Bible should be our authority for belief, yet we seem reluctant to wrestle with what the Bible may teach about the processes of ministry and leadership. As a result we tend to evaluate the content of sermons against the Bible, but we are less likely to use it to evaluate broader ministry and leadership processes. As long as the content of teaching can be supported from the Bible or tradition, there is little concern given to the processes involved. Whatever seems to work, or increase attendance or income, will often be accepted, without much thought about how it fits with the example of Jesus. The gap between the ministry of many Christians today and the ministry of Jesus is simply enormous. There is often little similarity between the activity of Jesus and that of many churches.

4. Why do the followers of Jesus take so little notice of Jesus' example and teaching? Christians often affirm that Jesus is a great teacher, but effectively ignore so much of his teaching or example. Many act as if Jesus' purpose on earth was simply to die for us, not to teach us anything about living. For example, Jesus had a lot to say about materialism and greed, but on that count most western Christians are virtually no different from anybody else. The birth, death and resurrection of Jesus figure prominently in evangelical teaching, while so many of the other things he did and said are neglected.

Jesus is the greatest leader who ever lived, yet today many who say they follow him don't follow his example as a leader. The first disciples were called by Jesus to follow him. They obeyed and became the leaders of the early church. What might it mean for Christian leaders today to follow Jesus? Read on!

ENDNOTES

1. Rost, Joseph Clarence, *Leadership for the Twenty-first Century,* Praeger Publishers 1991 pp. 42-43.

2. Luke 9:62

3. 1 Corinthians 11:1

change focused leadership

It's getting late and the leadership is still haggling over the latest church growth diagram. The same chart has been the focus of the last three meetings. This configuration of lines, arrows, rectangles and words outlines a plan for Community Christian Church to be transformed in the months and years ahead. Decades ago, this was a thriving church but in recent years it has seen declining attendance with little emphasis on discipleship and community outreach. There is always talk that change is just around the corner, that soon this church will join the list of church growth success stories. Three years ago a new strategic plan was developed and everything seemed to change: programs had new names, new committees were formed and there were even some new faces on some of the committees. It looked as if everything had changed, but, in the things that really mattered, nothing had changed. Attendance continued to decline, outreach to the community was still minimal and there was little evidence of discipleship growth in the members.

Does this sound familiar? Lots of activity in the name of change, but nothing of substance really changing? Meetings, strategic plans or diagrams can all be very useful. Sometimes the lack of thorough planning and a refusal to restructure can impede real change. However it is possible to do all these things and still not see the changes that are sought. And, all the time this theorising is going on, there are people in need of urgent help. Somehow it is hard to see Jesus making a priority of organisational mechanics.

Jesus obviously thought through what he was doing and he spent a lot of time talking with his disciples, but somehow his work transcends administrative procedures. Jesus was change-focused. He did not just make plans for change. Jesus saw real change take place; he was the greatest change-agent in history. The change-focused leadership of Jesus is evident in the story of the call of Simon, Andrew, James and John to be his disciples.

The story of the call of the first disciples

After John was put in prison, Jesus went into Galilee,
proclaiming the good news of God. 'The time has come,' he
said. 'The kingdom of God is near. Repent and believe the good
news!'

As Jesus walked beside the Sea of Galilee, he saw Simon and
his brother Andrew casting a net into the lake, for they were
fishermen. 'Come, follow me,' Jesus said, 'and I will make you
fishers of men.' At once they left their nets and followed him.

When he had gone a little farther, he saw James son of Zebedee
and his brother John in a boat, preparing their nets. Without
delay he called them, and they left their father Zebedee in the
boat with the hired men and followed him. Mark 1:14-20 (NIV)

It is urgent business and there is no time to waste. This is the
impression Mark creates as he tells the story of the call of Jesus'
first disciples. John the Baptist has been imprisoned and Jesus
launches into his public mission. First he begins to preach, 'The
kingdom of God is near. Repent and believe the good news.'
Then in Mark's very next sentence, Jesus approaches Simon and
Andrew to call them to 'follow'. The implication is that the call
to follow Jesus means to follow him by sharing in his mission.
They are to join Jesus in the urgent task of spreading the good
news. Their initial task is to accompany Jesus and learn from
him in a teacher-disciple relationship. Later they will take up the
message and mission of Jesus for themselves.

Simon and Andrew are fishermen and they are at work casting
a net, when Jesus approaches with the words, 'Follow me and
I will make you fishers of men'. To follow Jesus means, that
instead of catching fish, they will have a new occupation of
catching people for the Kingdom of God. The sovereignty
of Jesus pervades this story. It was Jesus who chose these
fishermen, not the fishermen who chose Jesus. Jesus also took
upon himself the responsibility of preparing these disciples for
their future ministry. He said, 'I will make you fishers of men',

pledging to shape these men into the leaders he wanted them to be. They would not just emerge naturally, nor would they be self-trained, they would be trained and developed by Jesus. It was Jesus who would transform these fishermen into fishers of men.

Mark describes the response of Simon and Andrew: 'at once they left their nets and followed him'. Jesus initiated a sudden call and these men made an immediate response. Their obedience was also very costly: 'they left their nets' which were the tools of their trade. Simon and Andrew gave up their fishing profession, status and economic security to follow Jesus. They made an immediate, uncompromising response to the call of Jesus.[1]

The story of the call of Simon and Andrew is followed by another story that is very similar. A little farther up the lake, Jesus sees James and John in their boat preparing their nets for the next fishing trip. 'Without delay' Jesus calls them and, like Simon and Andrew, their response is immediate and uncompromising. They leave behind their father Zebedee, regarding Jesus as more important than family ties. In leaving their boat they leave their business. It was a good business, too, because we are told that they left behind 'the hired men'. This was not just a father and son operation, but a good fishing business that employed a number of staff.

Francis Moloney[2] observed that both of these stories have a number of common features. The initiative is entirely on the side of Jesus. It is Jesus who calls and, in Mark's account, the disciples do not utter a single word but they respond immediately to the call to follow Jesus. They do not bargain or negotiate but simply obey. In both stories this obedience to the call of Jesus is costly, as they leave their businesses and careers to follow Jesus. The call of Jesus is sudden and obedience is immediate and uncompromising because this is an urgent mission. In this story a number of aspects of change-focused leadership can be identified.

The goal of leadership is change

'Follow me and I will make you fishers of men'. These words of Jesus indicate that he is intent on change and that transformational leadership was taking place. Transformational leadership is leadership that primarily works towards real change. Jesus was seeking change in two areas. Firstly, Jesus wanted the disciples to change into 'fishers of men'. Secondly, Jesus wanted other people to be given the opportunity to change through the influence of the disciples. That is the point of being 'fishers of men'. They were to fish for people so that those people could have the opportunity to live very different lives. The next chapter will deal more thoroughly with transformational leadership and it will be compared with other types of leadership. However four aspects of the transformational leadership of Jesus can be observed in this particular story.

The focus is transformation, not organisation

Preaching, teaching, healing, serving, answering questions, training disciples and debating with opponents: these are the things Jesus does in the gospel stories. He is out there doing it and other people are called to follow him and join him in his work. It is hardly boardroom-style leadership where people sit in a room and decide what other people should do. Jesus was out there in the community, taking the lead in all the things he wanted his followers to do. He got his hands dirty, touched lepers to bring healing, broke bread to feed the hungry, opened the scrolls of Scripture to explain their meaning and invested time in personal relationships to make disciples. People changed as a result. They were healed, fed, given hope and their beliefs and characters were transformed. Jesus' focus was change.

Jesus wanted his followers to also be concerned with change. He did not say, 'Follow me and I will put you on a committee or give you some position in my organisation'. He said, 'I will make you fishers of men'. Jesus was primarily concerned with transformation not organisation. He was more interested in engaging people in life-changing ways than managing an organisation. This is not to say that Jesus never concerned himself with management issues. The gospel writers depict Jesus at times delegating and coordinating activities (for example, Mark 6:39-44; Luke 22:8) but this was not his prime focus.

While organisation is important, it is not the main purpose of Christian ministry. Committees, minutes, budgets, strategic plans, reports and other management processes should support and empower the ministries of transformation. They should not become ends in themselves. Sometimes organisational procedures are given such an important place that they divert far too much time, energy and resources away from grass-roots ministry.

Damien was the youth leader of his church in his spare time. The leaders of the church decided that there would be a new central committee to coordinate and manage all the activities of the church and that the leaders of all the church ministries should attend. These were long meetings, held every week. Damien was very busy and only had two nights each week to devote to the youth ministry of the church. On those nights he would organise and run youth activities, visit families, counsel young people and coordinate and encourage the volunteer youth leaders who helped him. When the new central committee effectively took half the time Damien had available for youth ministry, he raised his concerns. He was told that the meetings were necessary and the central committee was so important that it must always be given priority.

After some time, Damien resigned from the committee because it diverted him and other people from the very ministries it was supposed to facilitate and encourage. His decision to resign created considerable conflict. He was treated as someone with misplaced priorities, who was letting the side down. Later, a large organisation with a hundred staff and thousands of volunteers employed Damien. The leadership meetings of the large organisation took a fraction of the time and achieved far more than the central committee at the church. Since that time the congregation of that church has continued to decline. There are no doubt lots of reasons for this but perhaps one of them was ministry management that diverted people from being fishers of men and women. Of course, it is important that ministry be managed. However, it is easy for committees to absorb far too much time and also provide a respectable escape from engaging in the lives of people. Organisation is important, but the focus should be on activities that help people change.

The emphasis is on qualitative change, not quantitative change

'Our goal is to double the number of members in three years.' 'We intend to plant two more churches in the next four years.' These are the sorts of goals churches frequently set, the way Christians often think of change. Sometimes our goals are just an excuse to stay exactly the same, but entice more people to join us in our unchanged state. Are these goals for change, or merely goals to have more people unchanged? Jesus did not seem to be concerned about numerical goals. He is never seen in the gospels setting goals to have a number of followers by a certain time. That does not mean that he was not concerned about reaching more people. He clearly wanted to take the gospel to others and he travelled from place to place in the process.

The point is that Jesus' goals were not focused on how many followers he had, but with what his followers were going to be like. The goal was not about numbers but about character and service. His command was 'repent' and his goal was to make his disciples into 'fishers of men'. He aimed for changed people who could help others change into followers of Jesus. The goal was not *more* people but *changed* people, and then *more changed* people. It is easy to set numerical goals and then embark on marketing exercises to expand our churches or religious organisations. It is much harder and more costly to explore how God wants us to change and how we can be more Christ-like. The change Jesus seeks is not more people conforming to us, but for us to be more conformed to Jesus. It is when we strive to be Christ-like in our outreach to others and lovingly respond to their physical, social, mental and spiritual needs that we engage in Biblical evangelism and not just settle for religious marketing. Biblical leadership requires that qualitative change have priority over quantitative growth.

The willingness to change is a prerequisite of leadership

The fishermen that Jesus approached by the Sea of Galilee were not at that stage, 'fishers of men'. They could not influence people to change in the ways Jesus had in mind. But what did Jesus say to them? 'I will make you fishers of men'. These words imply a process of leadership development. Here Jesus declared his intention to make these men into people who could influence others. This leadership development involved three years of intense, full time training by Jesus himself.

Leadership is usually not something that is acquired instantly. The knowledge, skills and attitudes required for leadership usually take considerable time and effort to develop. Occasionally I observe in people a keen desire to be leaders, but a reluctance for leadership development. Darren once told me how much he admired people who could understand and clearly explain the meaning of Bible passages in ways that helped people to change. He said that he would also like to be able to do that and asked me how he could learn these skills. I recommended as a start, a short course of about twenty hours that was being conducted by one of the Bible colleges. He quickly discounted the idea and I got the distinct impression that he was not interested in any training that would take more than a few minutes. Darren's attitude concerned me, because he seemed to believe that it was his right to teach even though he was not particularly willing to learn. The disciples did not instantly acquire leadership skills by some kind of spiritual magic. It took the discipline of years of learning and training.

Leaders begin with the end of a change process in mind

For a glimpse of the disciples once they became fishers of men, you have to read the early chapters of the book of Acts. That is where they are depicted helping the needy, healing, evangelising, teaching and leading. In the gospels the disciples are sent on mission where they begin to emerge as fishers of men (Mark 6:12), but it is in Acts that they are truly seen as men who are established in Christian ministry. Right from the beginning, Jesus had that in mind for the disciples.

Stephen Covey writes that effective people 'begin with the end in mind'.[3] Clearly at the beginning of his ministry with his disciples, Jesus had an end in mind, that they would be fishers of men. Jesus did not just aimlessly accept opportunities to help people and teach the Word of God. Jesus had a purpose. One of his purposes was to equip his disciples for ministry.

In my years of training Christian youth workers and youth leaders, I have discovered that some of them have no end in mind. Often they work very hard and make considerable sacrifices, and yet they don't really know what they are trying to achieve. As long as young people come to their programs and nothing bad happens, they are satisfied. Many have never thought about questions like, 'How do you want young people to be different as a result of coming to your youth program for three years?' I am sure that it's not only youth leaders who engage in ministry without any real purpose in mind. Avoid the trap of just running Christian programs for their own sake. Be intentional. Engage in ministry to achieve a purpose. Before you begin, have an end in mind.

Following is essential in the change process

Even though Jesus recruited disciples who would become leaders in the early church, he did not command them to lead but to follow. While it may be true that you cannot lead until you have learned to follow, these disciples did not follow merely as a preparation for leadership. Until the end of their lives these men saw themselves as followers of Jesus and taught others to do the same. Decades after this event, as an established leader of the church Peter wrote, 'to this you were called, because Christ suffered for you, leaving you an example, that you should follow in his steps'[4]. Genuine Christian leaders never cease to follow

Jesus, rather they lead others in following Jesus.

Jesus did not seem to appeal to leadership ambitions. On the other hand he censured his disciples for ambitions of greatness and the desire to be first. He taught them to be servants (Mark 10:35-45: Matthew 20: 20-28). He condemned the self-seeking attitudes and self-exulting behaviour of many of the leaders of Judaism (Matthew 23: 8-12). Jesus did not encourage the disciples to be eager to lead, but to follow. In the course of following Jesus, some of them emerged as leaders and they eventually led others in following Jesus.

We should not be too ambitious to be leaders. If, in the course of following Jesus, other people follow us, then we emerge as Christian leaders. But if we do not become leaders it does not matter, because we are not all called to lead but we are all called to follow. The research of Warren Bennis, who interviewed many recognised leaders, shows that they did not set out to lead but to express themselves.[5] Often, it is not that people decide to become leaders, but that they are concerned about issues in their various fields, and when they express their concerns, others agree and follow.

Followers are very important people. At times people have misunderstood leadership by focusing on the traits of people that they believed to be leaders. James Macgregor Burns took a different approach and emphasised that leadership involves a relationship between leaders and followers.[6] Burns wrote 'Leaders and followers are engaged in a common enterprise; they are dependent on each other, their fortunes rise and fall together, they share the results of planned change together.'[7]

We cannot begin to understand leadership unless we recognise the roles of followers. Leadership is not just about leaders. It is about leaders and followers working together to achieve some mutual purpose. Leaders cannot exist without followers and there must always be more followers than leaders. People become leaders when other people follow them. Rather than leaders making followers, in many ways it is followers who make leaders, by choosing to follow some people and not others. The idea that leaders are the people who count and that followers are second rate needs to be rejected. There is nothing wrong with being a follower. Followers are the backbone of leadership. Whatever is achieved in leadership is achieved not by leaders alone, but by the joint efforts of both leaders and followers.

Leadership is about change while management is about production

'How do you make people follow you?' Nathan anxiously asked me this question at a youth leader's training seminar. He explained that he had been appointed the youth leader of his church by the pastor, but the young people did not seem to take much notice of him. He felt responsible for the young people because he was their appointed leader and he was the one who was called to account for the youth ministry, but he explained that he had little influence over them. Nathan obviously expected that when he was appointed 'Youth Leader' all the young people would automatically follow him, but he was totally confused when they followed another young man who was not the official youth leader.

This incident raises the following questions:

- Can you make people leaders simply by appointing them?

- What are the advantages and limitations of being in a leadership position?

- How do people become leaders?

- What is leadership anyway?

I believe that the answers to these questions rest in the distinction between leadership and management. Many become confused in their efforts to understand leadership because they start with people they recognise as leaders and then label everything these people do as leadership. They follow a similar process with management. This assumes that leaders do leadership all the time while managers do management all the time. In practice, many do both leadership and management at different times and perhaps sometimes even do both concurrently. It's not helpful to put people in boxes labelled 'leader' as if everything these people do is leadership, even eating and sleeping. It is more helpful to try to understand the nature of leadership. Similarly, it is more helpful to try to understand the nature of management than to put people in boxes that we label 'manager'. Particular people could still be referred to as leaders or managers, but a clearer understanding of these issues is gained by exploring when leadership and management is occurring than by starting with individuals and working back.

The following definitions by Joseph Rost make clear distinctions between leadership and management.[8]

> 'Leadership is an influence relationship among leaders and followers who intend real changes that reflect mutual purposes.'

> 'Management is an authority relationship between at least one manager and one subordinate who coordinate their activities to produce and sell particular goods and/or services.'

These definitions allow Rost to highlight four fundamental differences between leadership and management. Let us leave the story in Mark's gospel for a while and explore what Rost has to teach us about leadership and management. Then we will come back to the gospels and apply this to Jesus.

Leadership is an influence relationship while management is an authority relationship

Leadership and management involve different types of relationships. Management involves an authority relationship. Managers hold positions of authority where they guide activities and maintain control. Subordinates do not have to agree with managers but they must substantially comply or leave the organisation. This does not mean that management is always harsh. Managers might be quite sensitive and respectful and negotiate in a very pleasant manner, but in the end they can demand obedience. At the bottom line it is about authority not influence.

Leadership often has no authority and the people who exercise leadership sometimes have no official position in an organisation whereby they can demand obedience. Leadership is about influence. It occurs when people act willingly, convinced that they are doing what they want to do, even if it is at the suggestion of somebody else. Leadership does not use threats, coercion or enticements. If people are being forced then leadership is not occurring. Followers do not have to do what their leaders say but they willingly follow.

Nathan in the story above was confused because he did not understand this distinction. The role of Youth Leader is a management position within churches. Even though the term 'leader' is employed, youth leaders are usually, in reality, managers of youth programs. This gives them some authority but it does not guarantee any influence. Nathan was confused and threatened because somebody else had influence and was exercising leadership even though that person was not the official youth leader.

Leadership involves leaders and followers while management involves managers and subordinates

Managers are obeyed while leaders are followed. Managers have subordinates not followers while leaders have followers not subordinates. Managers depend on their position in the organisation for their authority. If they lose their position they lose their authority. Leaders do not depend on their position but their influence. If they lose their influence they lose their leadership.

Managers are appointed but leaders are not appointed. Leaders emerge and they can emerge at any level in an organisation or community. Nelson Mandela exercised leadership even when he was a prisoner and had no authority over anyone. Subordinates often have no say in the selection of their managers but leaders can only be leaders because their followers choose to follow them. This is the ultimate test of leadership: to lead is to be followed. If no one is following, you are not leading no matter what your talents, qualifications or position.

Nathan above figured that he was the only one in the group who could exercise leadership because he was the appointed leader. Leadership can emerge from anyone in the group and in many groups the person exercising leadership changes all the time. Someone has an idea and everybody follows until someone else leads the group in another direction. All this can happen quite unconsciously and without any change in the official 'leadership' position. This is normal and healthy but unfortunately many in official leadership positions are uneasy when others have influence, seeing it as a threat to their authority.

Leadership intends real changes while management produces or sells goods and/or services

Management is about production and/or sales while leadership attempts real change. In industry the task of management is to produce and/or sell goods and services. The same is true for the management of Christian ministry. Church services and other programs have to be organised and sometimes goods such as literature must be produced. These need to be financed and promoted, or made accessible to the intended recipients.

Leadership is not about production or sales, but change. This is not just superficial change in programs or organisational structures but real change in the attitudes, values, beliefs and behaviours in people, groups or communities. Even if the attempt at change is not successful, leadership is occurring whenever leaders and followers are working together with the intention of creating real change.

While I would agree with Rost on this point, I suspect that leadership is primarily about values. Leaders push for change because they hold certain values. It is not that they want change for the sake of change, but they promote values that demand change in nations, communities or people's lives. Management is about production while leadership is about values that promote change. Good management then is about the efficiency of production, while good leadership is about the clarity and validity of the values that promote change. One of the ironies of this is that those who often claim to be Christian leaders, do not direct their energy at bringing about changes that are consistent with the values of the kingdom of God, instead they do everything they can to maintain the status quo. Leadership is never satisfied with the status quo; it strives for change.

Leadership reflects mutual purposes while management focuses on coordinating activities

Management is about coordinating activities to produce or sell products, goods or services (like ministry programs and literature). Leadership is occurring when leaders and followers agree that something needs to be changed and they work together for that change. That is, the leaders and followers develop a mutual purpose for change.

This summarises the differences that Rost sees between leadership and management. However a few clarifications are in order. Firstly, although management and leadership have been separated above for the sake of analysis, as was stated before, they are not mutually exclusive and often both operate concurrently. The game of soccer involves running and kicking. Soccer players might kick or run, but often they are kicking and running at the same time. Although kicking and running are quite different functions, a soccer player often does both at once. Similarly someone in a management position could be doing leadership as well as management at the same time. When subordinates willingly work with managers to create real change as well as produce or sell their goods or services, leadership may well be occurring as well as management.

Secondly, while management and leadership are different they are both necessary and important. Some people suggest that leadership is good but management is bad, or at least inferior. Management is good. It is good to have wages and rent paid, facilities booked, activities coordinated and finances in order. Management and leadership are different but that does not mean one is more important than the other. It is possible to have good management and poor or no leadership and it is also possible to have poor management and good leadership. In the former, everything is organised and runs smoothly but there is no challenge to change and the system is ruled by the status quo. In the latter there is vision and people are trying to address needs but things are disorganised and chaotic. Both leadership and management should be valued.

Before reading further, consider the scenario on pages 44-46.

Thirdly, the use of authority or coercion is not necessarily wrong. There are times when strong action is necessary. However the use of coercion or authority indicates that leadership is not occurring at that time. It might be management that is occurring but it is not leadership. Some instances of coercion, though, are completely unnecessary and have more in common with bullying than valid management.

When we understand the difference between leadership and management a lot of things start to make sense. We can see why a person who is not an appointed leader might have far more influence than the official leaders. We can see why giving orders is effective in some circumstances but useless in others. We can see why people who are often the most influential are sometimes lower down in the organisational structures. We can also see why leadership is such a tricky business. Training, position and ability cannot guarantee that anyone will exercise leadership.

Now let's come back to the gospel stories and reflect on them in the light of Joseph Rost's descriptions of leadership and management.

...to page 50

Imagine you have recently accepted the task of organising and leading a youth camp. This camp has been running for several years. There is always some turnover, but it has an established leadership team and attracts a regular group of teenagers. So far nothing has been booked and nothing planned for the next camp.

The stated purpose of the camp over the years has been fellowship and Bible teaching.

Most of the campers have Christian parents, regularly attend church and claim to be Christians. At camp they willingly attend the Bible teaching sessions and join in the program. An anonymous survey conducted last year showed that about half of them regularly read their Bibles and pray. Most wrote that their main ambition is to get rich. You have noticed a reluctance to get involved in any kind of service or response to the needy. Last year a couple of Asian migrants attended the camp and were clearly made unwelcome. Some of the campers are concerned about these values and behaviours and willingly embrace the challenges of Christian discipleship. Most of the leadership team is also concerned but they are at a loss to know what to do.

Task 1

List the management roles and tasks involved in organising and running this camp.

For example, What goods and services are to be produced or sold? What activities need to be coordinated? How will authority be maintained? How will your duty of care responsibilities be carried out?

Task 2

Identify the leadership issues and opportunities involved.

For example, What changes in values, beliefs and behaviours need to be identified and worked for? How could these young people be influenced to change?

Here are some of the management roles and tasks involved in organising and running this camp.

Facilities need to be booked, catering and transport arranged and brochures printed and distributed. A program needs to be planned and a team of leaders recruited and trained. The formal Christian input must be organised, which may involve inviting a speaker and a music team. Other issues to be considered include first aid, duty of care, procedures for responding to unacceptable behaviour, the registration process, pastoral care and the general atmosphere and ethos of the camp.

Here are some of the leadership issues and opportunities that need to be worked out. Obviously some young people are very committed to Jesus. How can they be helped to develop further in their knowledge, attitudes and service? Many of them go to church regularly but hardly ever read their Bibles or pray. Are they just living off the faith of their parents? What sort of relationship do they have with Jesus? How can these young people develop a more consistent relationship with Jesus or perhaps even encounter Jesus for themselves for the first time? There is a third group that regularly participate, read their Bibles and pray but this seems to make little difference in their attitudes to others. How can they put the teaching of the Bible into practice in their own lives? How can their materialism, racism and lack of compassion be addressed? They embrace the grace, mercy and compassion of God but how can they be helped to pass that on to others? In what ways can this camp be used to help these young people change? How do we want them to be different as a result of this camp? It may not be wise to try to tackle all these issues in the one camp but leadership requires striving for real change.

It is clear that both tasks are important: both the management and leadership issues should be considered. Good management will ensure that all the aspects of the camp are planned and coordinated in a way that ensures the enjoyment, health and welfare of the young people who attend. The process of leadership will consider the values and beliefs that need to be promoted and will strive to see changes take place in the lives of those young people.

...from page 47

How would we describe the activities of Jesus in the gospel stories? Is it leadership or management? As stated before there were times when Jesus performed management functions, delegating tasks and coordinating activities (Mark 6:39; Luke 22:8). However the dominant dynamic in these stories is more leadership than management, and the leadership characteristics identified by Rost are clearly seen in the relationship between Jesus and his disciples. A major theme in this story is *following*, 'they left their nets and followed him'. This is clearly a leader-follower relationship. As identified earlier, Jesus also had change in mind. There was a clear focus on transformation. He was calling people to change, to 'repent and believe'. He wanted to change the disciples into fishers of men. It was in this context that the disciples joined Jesus in his mission and shared his purpose.

The relationship between Jesus and his disciples was also not based on coercion, threats or intimidation. The disciples loved Jesus and willingly followed him. Jesus obviously had great authority and the authority of Jesus is one of the major themes of Mark's gospel. At times Jesus did command the disciples, but we are not given the impression that they were coerced, intimidated or paid to follow Jesus. Even though Jesus had the authority of the Son of God, and at times issued commands, the overall relationship was based on influence, not coercion. Jesus is a great example of a person who had authority, but generally preferred influence over coercion. The disciples often obeyed Jesus. Sometimes they disobeyed. But at the bottom line, they followed. They often followed him poorly but they followed him willingly. This is the stuff of leadership.

It is God who calls people into a change process

'The beginning of the gospel about Jesus Christ, the Son of God.' It was with these words that Mark began his gospel. So readers of Mark's Gospel know something that may not be known by some of the people we read about in his book. As we read these stories about Jesus, we do so as readers who have already been informed that this is about the Son of God. The disciples and other characters in the story may struggle to understand Jesus, but we have been told that he is the Son of God.

We can only guess what these fishermen understood about Jesus at this time. Jesus had met Simon and Andrew before, along with two other disciples, Philip and Nathanael. The story is recorded in John 1:29-51 when these four men were involved with John the Baptist, who was baptising at Bethany on the Jordan River. In John's story they had a number of encounters with Jesus and various people referred to Jesus as 'the Lamb of God', 'the Messiah' and 'the Son of God'. It is hard to know how the disciples understood these terms in their early experiences of Jesus. It is clear that they remained quite confused about what it meant to be the Messiah until after Jesus' resurrection.

We know that Mark's story about the call of the fisherman beside the Sea of Galilee occurred sometime after the story recorded in John's gospel, because it happened 'after John was put in prison'. So when Jesus approached Simon and Andrew beside the lake with the call to 'follow me', it was not as someone who was unknown. They had met Jesus before and John's story indicates that they realised that Jesus was special. Whatever their understanding of Jesus, they would not have understood that Jesus is the Son of God in the same way as Mark's original readers. The authority that Jesus has, as the Son of God, is clearly demonstrated in the early chapters of Mark. Jesus taught with authority (Mark 1:22), and demonstrated his authority over demons (Mark 1:27), disease (Mark 1:32), sin (Mark 2:10) and the wind and sea (Mark4: 41). Jesus is no ordinary person: he has supernatural authority.

This raises some important issues about the leadership of Jesus, at least in the mind of the readers. Jesus had a special relationship with God and supernatural authority. While Jesus had leadership qualities that can be observed in others, some people also followed him because of his unique relationship with God and his extraordinary authority. This also has implications for the eventual leadership of these disciples. In this story, the Son of God called them into his service. Initially these men were followers of Jesus but they were included in the group of twelve apostles who eventually became leaders of the early church. Mark does not depict these disciples in their early experience of Jesus as ambitious men grasping at their big chance for leadership. Rather they are chosen by Jesus to be 'fishers of men'. They had no idea at that time where it would all end.

In the Bible there are many examples where God calls particular people into leadership or ministry roles. Peter, Andrew, James and John are just four of them. There is no shortage of people in the modern world who claim that God has called them to some special task, ministry or leadership role. I have encountered many people who claimed that God called them to a particular ministry and they have done a good job in a responsible manner. However I have encountered other people who have claimed to be called by God and have performed very poorly. I know others who said that God clearly called them to a particular ministry but they only lasted a few weeks or months.

The difficulty is not whether God can call people, as the Son of God called these fishermen, but how to deal with people who claim to be called by God. The claim to be called by God is of course, almost an impossible claim to test. How are we to know if such claims are true? When God has called people, how is their accountability to be managed? To what degree can people disagree with them without resisting God himself? What happens to people who question whether or not God really has called them?

These questions are important because there are people who seem to think that their claim that God has called them, means that they are exempt from accountability and cannot be resisted, questioned or corrected. The Son of God himself called these four disciples yet on many occasions they were questioned, corrected and rebuked. The gospel stories clearly show that Jesus, who called them, did not believe that such a call made them infallible or exempted them from correction or accountability. It is also worth noting that the disciples accepted such correction. The disciples made many mistakes despite their call and they had much to learn. The call of God to biblical leadership always includes a call to be teachable, accountable and humble. It is not a call to infallibility, freedom from failure or protection from criticism. God recognises our weaknesses yet calls us all the same, to be involved in his great work of transformation.

Another problem is the assumption that involvement in any ministry should always follow a supernatural experience in which God calls us into that particular service. There have been trained, responsible people who have applied for ministry roles but have been denied positions because they could not describe a particular call to that specific ministry. Some Bible characters did receive special calls to particular ministries but that does not mean that God always works that way. The Bible teaches that we should all love God and our neighbours. We do not need a special call to do that. The world is a very needy place and there are plenty of opportunities. There is nothing wrong with making prayerful, considered decisions about how we should be involved. The Bible contains many examples of people responding to situations without special messages from God telling them what to do. This is not to say that God does not call people to specific ministry roles but it does not always happen that way.

The need for change is urgent

A sense of urgency pervades Mark's story. Phrases like 'at once' and 'without delay' convey messages of quick and decisive actions. Furthermore Mark writes in a concise, active style that creates an impression of urgency. Everything seems to happen quickly, as if there is no time to waste. Jesus' task of preaching the arrival of the kingdom of God and the need for repentance is of utmost importance. The needs are pressing and the disciples are called to assist Jesus in this urgent mission.

We live in a desperately needy world and many Christians need to recapture the urgency of Jesus. This is not the type of urgency that is clumsy and impatient, where there is no time to plan, prepare or train. It is not the type of urgency that uses dishonesty or exploitation to gain short-term advances. It is an urgency that has as its foundation the immense needs of human beings and the heart of God who longs to restore and include them within his kingdom. There is no time to waste. The needs are great, the opportunities are abundant and the mission is urgent. Let's get on with it.

ENDNOTES

1. Moloney, Francis J. Disciples and Prophets, Darton, Longman and Todd Ltd, 1980.

2. Moloney, Francis J Leadership in the Christian Scriptures, A series of lectures presented at the Australian Catholic University, Brisbane, Queensland, Australia, 1999.

3. Covey, Stephen R The Seven Habits of Highly Effective People, The Business Library, 1989, pp. 95-144.

4. 1Peter 2:21

5. Bennis, Warren On Becoming a Leader, Addison-Wesley Publishing Company, 1989, pp. 5-6.

6. Burns, James Macgregor Leadership, Harper and Row, 1978, pp. 18-21.

7. Burns, James Macgregor Leadership, Harper and Row, 1978, pp. 426.

8. Rost, Joseph Clarence Leadership for the Twenty-first Century, Praeger Publishers, 1991, pp. 101-152.

people-centred leadership

Beth's story

Beth's sister died on a Wednesday morning. She had first been diagnosed with cancer some eight months before, and within a few weeks the family knew it was terminal. Beth was very busy at work when she received the call that her sister had passed away. She went home as soon as she could, and spent some time comforting her elderly parents and others in the extended family. There were phone calls, visits and arrangements to be made and relatives soon started turning up for the funeral from far and wide. In the midst of all this, Beth had to return to work to sort out some urgent matters. Suddenly it was Friday afternoon, time for the funeral. Beth was encouraged to see some old friends that she had not seen for a long time and comforted by the kind words spoken in the service.

After the funeral Beth arrived home feeling very flat and drained. Then she remembered that it was youth group night. With everything that had been going on she had forgotten - and she was the leader! Fortunately she had done some preliminary preparation early in the week so she quickly ate some food and hurried off to the church. Her head was in a muddle and the last thing she felt like doing that night was leading a youth group, but she was stuck with it. She knew she should be somewhere else, but she couldn't leave that group of young people unsupervised. The pastor had not made any contact with Beth and nor had any of the other leaders of the church. No one had asked if they should arrange for someone else to look after youth group that night.

Beth's depression began to turn to anger as parents, many of them church leaders, dropped off their teenagers. They smiled and waved, driving away as soon as their offspring jumped out of the car. They knew what had happened that day yet no one offered to help in any way. She could not escape the conclusion that these church leaders didn't care a great deal about her.

Beth felt used. Some weeks later she expressed to one of the church leaders that she was disappointed that none of them had contacted her when her sister died. It would have been appreciated, she said, if they'd arranged for someone else to lead youth group on the night of the funeral. The response was, that as the youth leader it was Beth's responsibility to find a replacement if she could not be there. This was not an isolated incident; it was part of a pattern. It was not long after this that Beth left that church.

Which Christian leaders have you found most helpful over the years? What were they like? The first to come to my mind are the leaders who really cared about me and did not treat me as someone who was there just to do a job or make up the numbers. However, they were also people who had a viewpoint and would not just agree with me on anything. They had a good grasp of God's Word, they knew what they believed and helped me to think about my faith and apply it to my life. They did not place themselves above me but operated on my level. They were people-centred.

There are healthy as well as unhealthy ways to be people-centred. I respected people who influenced me but hated attempts to manipulate me. I was frustrated by those who maintained tradition at all costs, yet I was suspicious of those who merely trampled on tradition, because both extremes fail to adequately value the people involved. I was annoyed when group goals were sacrificed just to keep certain people happy. In many of these situations the leaders involved would claim to be people-centred, and they could name the people at the centre of their concern, yet it was often quite twisted. 'Mrs. Wilson just cannot cope with change so we can't do that.' 'Personally I don't agree either, but Robert supports us financially and we can't afford to upset him.' 'Don't talk to me about ethics. It doesn't matter if it is illegal, we stand to make a lot of money out of this and it will all go to reaching young people for Christ.' (The CEO of a Christian organisation really did say that to me.) To be people-centred means far more than to be able to think of someone or some group that gets what they want or might receive an advantage from a certain line of action.

Let's explore the ways in which Jesus was people-centred in the story of the call of Peter in Luke 5:1-11.

Luke's story of the call of Peter

One day as Jesus was standing by the Lake of Gennesaret, with the people crowding around him and listening to the Word of God, he saw at the water's edge two boats, left there by the fishermen, who were washing their nets. He got into one of the boats, the one belonging to Simon, and asked him to put out a little from the shore. Then he sat down and taught the people from the boat.

When he has finished speaking, he said to Simon, 'Put out into deep water, and let down the nets for a catch.'

Simon answered, 'Master, we've worked hard all night and haven't caught anything. But because you say so, I will let down the nets.' When they had done so, they caught such a large number of fish that their nets began to break. So they signalled to their partners in the other boat to come and help them, and they came and filled both boats so full that they began to sink. When Simon Peter saw this, he fell at Jesus' knees and said, 'Go away from me, Lord; I am a sinful man!' For he and all his companions were astonished at the catch of fish they had taken, and so were James and John, the sons of Zebedee, Simon's partners.

Then Jesus said to Simon, 'Don't be afraid; from now on you will catch men.' So they pulled their boats up on the shore, left everything and followed him. Luke 5:1-11.

An issue for the more thoughtful reader

ONE EVENT OR TWO?

Is this story the same incident or a different incident from that recorded in Mark 1? In Luke's account, Jesus used Peter's boat to sit in while he taught and there is also the miraculous catch of fish. Did Mark simply omit these aspects, or were there two different events? Both options are possible. A comparison of Mark's account of the death and resurrection of Jesus with Luke's account shows that Luke included many things that Mark left out such as the trial by Herod, the conversion of the thief on the cross and Jesus' appearance to two disciples on the road to Emmaus. Luke often gave more details than Mark and so this may well be the same incident. For the purposes of this book it makes little difference.

While Mark's story emphasises the immediate, uncompromising response to the call of Jesus, Luke's account provides a window into what is going on inside Peter and the inner changes taking place. Peter's response is slower. He develops an awareness of his own brokenness and lack of understanding, an awareness which culminates in his surrender to Jesus and willingness to follow him.

Have you ever had to escape a big crowd of people? This story opens with Jesus protecting himself from a crowd he was teaching by the Lake of Gennesaret (Galilee). Nearby there are two boats belonging to fishermen washing their nets after a night's fishing. Jesus gets into Simon's boat, asks him to put out a little from shore, then sits down in the teaching position of a Jewish rabbi and speaks to the crowd. It is in this context that Jesus calls the disciples. The crowd is pressing in around Jesus, so eager to hear the word of God that Jesus has to take action to give himself space. Jesus calls his disciples to help in the task of catching these and other people for God.

When Jesus has finished teaching he commands Simon, 'Put out into deep water, and let down your nets for a catch'. Simon replies that they had worked hard all night and had not caught anything but because Jesus said so he would let down the nets. Leon Morris suggests that there may be an implied rebuke in Simon's words.[1] 'Night was considered the best time for fishing, and Peter may be suggesting that when experts, fishing at the right time, had caught nothing, it was useless to try at the request of a carpenter.' Simon is full of his own knowledge. He should have know better because, in Luke's account, Jesus had just healed his mother-in-law (Luke 4:38), but Peter's willingness to act shows that Jesus cannot be ignored on any subject. Peter calls Jesus 'Master' and obeys: he might not agree but he does obey.

The result is a huge catch of fish. The meaning of the Greek text is that the nets were actually breaking under the load, not just threatening to break. Their partners come to their aid with the other boat and they fill the boats so full that both boats begin to sink. Simon is overwhelmed and not just with the size of the catch: there is a new awareness of Jesus and himself. Verse 8 is the only occasion in Luke's gospel where Peter is called 'Simon Peter'. Prior to verse 8 he is called Simon and after verse 8 he is usually referred to by his Christian title, Peter. However this is the moment of Simon's conversion: this is the point where Simon the fisherman becomes Peter the disciple. According to Francis Moloney this was Peter's breaking point.[2]

> At the miracle Simon's self-assertiveness crumbles. Luke cunningly no longer calls him 'Simon', but 'Simon Peter', adding the Christian title 'Peter', as he crumbles completely before the one who confronts him. He repents and believes: 'He fell down at Jesus' knees, saying, "Depart from me for I am a sinful man"'. It is thus, as a believer, conscious of his own weakness and need before the person of Jesus, that Peter is made a disciple.

Peter's confession of being 'a sinful man' is not a confession of a particular sin but a general sense of unworthiness before Jesus. Peter and the other fishermen, are astonished at the size of the catch, particularly given that it was the wrong time and wrong place to catch fish. 'This was a miracle in Peter's own area of expertise. He knew fishing; and therefore he knew what this haul implied.'[3] It amazes, not just Peter, but the whole group of professional fishermen. Peter's reaction shows that he interprets it as a miraculous display of divine power.

Peter tells Jesus to 'go away', but Jesus does not go away. What eventuates is that Peter follows Jesus. Despite Peter's confession of sinfulness, Jesus responds with a statement of acceptance and even commission: 'Don't be afraid; from now on you will catch men'. The Greek word translated 'men' means human beings not just men and the word translated 'catch' is not the normal word used for catching fish but it means 'to capture alive'. So Jesus is saying that instead of catching fish to be killed and eaten, Peter is now going to catch living men and women.

In Luke's story there is no call from Jesus to 'follow me', yet the response of the disciples is similar to the response in Mark's account, 'They left everything and followed him'. Jesus speaks directly to Simon, but a number of others also become Jesus' disciples. They had just had the best catch of fish in their lives but the catch was not as important as what it taught them about Jesus. So they leave their boats, security and status and follow Jesus.

This is a story about crossing boundaries. Peter leaves the shore as a fisherman to become a disciple in the 'deep water'. It contains parallels with stories Luke would write in The Acts of the Apostles telling of Peter catching men and women alive for the Kingdom of God. In these stories Peter would again and again launch out into 'deep water' and see astounding things happen in unlikely situations.

Jesus demonstrates several aspects of people-centred leadership in this story.

Christian leadership meets human need

In the midst of a crowd, Jesus recruited Peter and his friends to help in the task of catching men and women for the kingdom of God. Jesus was responding to human need and Peter and the other fishermen joined him in that task. It seems obvious that Christian leadership should focus on meeting human need but the needs of people are often overridden by other concerns. For some it is all about running programs. For them, at various times in the week or year, certain programs must be run. The faithful dutifully attend and the 'leaders' routinely organise programs to entertain and fill the lives of the faithful. Often little thought is given to the needs of these people and even less to how they might be equipped to address the needs of others. In this line of thinking it is the religious programs that are all important. The people exist to maintain the programs and the programs have little connection with the needs of people. Jesus placed little or no emphasis on programs. Apart from attending the synagogues, organised programs had little place in Jesus' ministry. The needs of people though, were very important. We need the same priorities. People don't exist to attend programs and programs are only valid when they address the needs of people.

The desire to use ministry gifts can also deflect from people-centred leadership. There is no question that it is good for people to be able to recognise their abilities and to exercise and develop their ministry gifts. However gifts and abilities must be kept in proper perspective. Our gifts and abilities are to be used to meet the needs of other people; they are not ends in themselves, to be pursued for their own sake. Jesus recruited Peter in response to the needs of human beings and not as a response to any need those disciples may have had to exercise ministry or leadership gifts. Primarily it is not that Jesus saw in Peter some great gifts that needed expression, rather, he saw people in great need and he recruited Peter to use his gifts and abilities to meet those needs. Of course it is true that Peter had gifts and abilities that once developed, proved to be very useful. The issue is not whether gifts and abilities should be used, but to what end. The driving question should not be 'When and how do I get to use my gifts?' but 'What are the human needs that we face and how can my mix of gifts and abilities best address those needs?' Preachers should not preach just to use their preaching gifts. Music should not be included in a program just to allow musicians to use their talents. Gifts and abilities should be always directed at meeting the needs of human beings and helping people to worship and serve God. Leaders are raised not primarily to exercise their skills and abilities, but to use them to address human need.

Christian leadership engages human frailty

This story ends with the words: 'they left everything and followed him'. Luke's story adds new dimensions to the relationship between leading and following. To follow Jesus not only involves following Jesus as leader but the surrender of our lives to him to shape our values, beliefs and actions. The starting point is repentance and humility. It is as Peter crumbles before Jesus in repentance that he is set apart for leadership. As Peter is made aware of his sinfulness, he is embraced by the grace of Jesus in which he not only finds acceptance but he is chosen for a task.

Here is another aspect of the leadership of Jesus that is unique. The behaviour of Peter and Jesus goes far beyond that which would normally be expected in a leader-follower relationship. Followers do not normally crumble in repentance before their leaders nor is this a practice that is likely to be recommended. Peter's behaviour would probably be considered unhealthy if this was somebody other than Jesus, but Luke has already told us that Jesus is 'the Son of God' (Luke 1:35). Therefore this display of brokenness and repentance is not just acceptable but necessary. To be a follower of Jesus means to give one's life to Jesus in a way that would not usually be expected of the followers of other leaders. Jesus is no ordinary person and he is entitled to a response that goes beyond the ordinary.

In this story Peter displays an awareness of his inadequacy and need of grace that is essential for Christian leadership. The gospel writers tend to depict Peter as naturally self-assertive. This would be a strength in his later ministry (Acts 4:13,29,31) but he had to be moulded by Jesus so that he would no longer merely assert Peter's agenda but that of his master.

Three points need to be made

Jesus is different and in some ways we cannot be like him

There are aspects of the leadership of Jesus that we can observe in other leadership relationships and put into practice to some extent in our own lives. There are other aspects of Jesus' leadership that are unique because he is the Son of God. He can do things that other human beings cannot do and Jesus' followers respond to him in ways that they should not respond to anyone else. Other leaders are followed, but Jesus is also worshipped.

Christian leadership begins with recognition of our own frailty

Before Jesus gave Peter the task of catching people for the kingdom of God, he brought him to his knees. It was in repentance and humility that Peter was set apart for leadership. As Peter was made aware of his own sinfulness, he was embraced by the grace of God. Like Peter, our starting point in Christian leadership is the recognition that Jesus is the Son of God and we are frail and sinful. Christian leaders do not have it all together. We have all failed in many ways and we continue to fall short. Christian ministry should always be exercised in the awareness of our need of grace.

Christian leadership involves helping others recognise their frailty

Peter did not need to measure up before he could follow Jesus but he did need to repent. Peter was accepted by Jesus but also pointed in a new direction. On the one hand Peter was accepted just as he was, but on the other hand, he realised that his life needed to go in a new direction. People are frail and sinful so they need to be treated with grace, yet this goes hand in hand with a call to repentance that requires surrender to Jesus and a willingness to please him. To engage human frailty means to help people embrace the grace of God and seek his new directions for their lives.

Different human relationships produce different types of leadership

Brian and David both consider themselves to be successful, people-centred pastors. In some ways they are similar, yet the types of leadership they exercise are very different. As you read their profiles below try to identify the key differences.

Brian is the pastor who is keenly aware of the various interest groups in his church. There is a ladies group which runs events like flower shows and fashion parades. These raise profile in the community and valuable funds for the missions budget. The ladies enjoy organising these events and Brian is careful to promote them and ensure that the group is given priority in the use of facilities and the church calendar. He knows that in return he can count on these ladies to cater for other church functions and assist with the cleaning and decoration of the facilities.

Brian learnt very quickly that it is important for a few of the men to be noticed. He gives these men prominent roles to perform in church services and they always support Brian in the decision-making bodies of the church. Some other men are coaches of the church soccer club that plays in the denominational competition. The club has three teams that involve about 50 boys. About six of these boys come from church families and another two come to youth group. The rest have no contact with Brian's church but the soccer competition only allows teams to compete that have a sponsoring church. The church's sponsorship of the soccer club ensures the support of those church families involved in soccer.

The church youth group has about 25 young people who attend regularly, of which 20 are from church families. Unfortunately the pattern over the years has been for young people to drop out of church or join another church once they get to about 18 years

of age. Consequently there are very few people in the church between 19 and 35 years of age. The young people who transfer to
other churches say that they did not like the very traditional services and wanted a more contemporary style of service. Whenever
changing the service has been raised, most of the people over 40
years of age object. Brian can see the point of view of the young
people who leave but he cannot see any way to solve the problem. Sometimes Brian finds it hard to cater for all interest groups
in the church but overall he is happy with his performance. The
budget is balanced every year and, when Brian's current term
comes to an end, he is confident that the congregation will vote
for him to be retained.

David wants his ministry to reflect biblical values and he has
identified discipleship and mission as areas of ministry that need
emphasis. On the whole, his congregation share his vision which
is to grow together to know and love God, to share God's love
with their local community and to seek to respond to the needs
of the world. Out of these convictions they have together developed programs that are carefully designed to help the church
achieve its goals.

The church services fall into two broad categories. Most services involve Bible teaching and are designed to encourage the
growth and discipleship of Christians. Other services are carefully designed for those who are new in their exposure to the
Christian faith. Home groups are attended by 80% of the church
members, the aim of the groups being discipleship development
and the nurture of new converts. David has trained the youth
leaders. They aim to provide a youth ministry that reflects these
values of discipleship and mission, expressed in the context of
youthful fellowship and fun. The members of the congregation
are actively involved in the local community. They can be found
in schools and community groups that respond to the needs of
youth, the homeless, elderly, disabled and poor.

Most of the members of the church agree with David's direction
and they support him in his ministry. Often it is hard to distin-
guish what David does from what the congregation does. They
are all absorbed in the same purpose. In fact this is why they

called David as their pastor in the first place: they agreed with his emphasis on discipleship and mission and his concern to be biblical.

However they have plenty of problems. Some people in the community do not like the influence these Christians have developed and at times they have been slandered. There is also a minority within the church who believe that the past traditions of the church should be given more emphasis and that too much is done for outsiders. There is ongoing conflict with these people and some have threatened to leave several times.

Before you proceed, consider these questions:

In what ways are Brian and David similar in how they exercise leadership?

In what ways are Brian and David different in how they exercise leadership?

What are the strengths and weaknesses of Brian's leadership?

What are the strengths and weaknesses of David's leadership?

Which of these two men exercises leadership most like that of Jesus? Explain

In your own leadership are you more like Brian or more like David? Explain. In what ways would you like to change?

Brian and David are examples of two main types of leadership that were identified and described by James Macgregor Burns.[4]

Transactional leadership

Transactional leadership is the most common type of leadership. It is typified by transactions or exchanges. This is the type of leadership commonly encountered in politics where certain government services (like lower taxes or better roads) are offered in exchange for votes. Of the two pastors described, Brian is the example of transactional leadership. He gives various individuals and groups in the church what they want in exchange for some kind of support or service.

In transactional leadership, the leaders and followers have different but related goals. For example, it might not be part of Brian's goal to have flower shows, fashion parades and a soccer club. These reflect the goals of other people. However by giving other people what they want, Brian gains their support and gets things he wants. So the individual goals of the various parties are advanced but there is no mutual goal. While the goals of these parties are different, they are related in that they focus on a common process, which in Brian's case, is the running of a church. In other cases the common process could be the running of a business, organisation or government.

Transformational leadership

Transformational leadership is a less common but a more powerful type of leadership. It aims at transformation as it attempts to create real change in individuals, groups, communities or societies. Of the two pastors described, David is the example of transformational leadership. David and his followers are working to create change in their own lives, their church, the community and the world. They want to become more like Jesus, help others come to know Jesus and transform their community into one that is a better reflection of the values of Jesus.

It is the *nature of the goals* that separates transformational leadership from transactional leadership. While in transactional leadership the parties have different but related goals, in transformational leadership both leaders and followers mutually share the same goals. David shares the same goals as most of the members of his church and these goals aim at transformation: real, significant change.

Another difference is that while transactional leadership focuses on a process (like running a church, government etc), transformational leadership concentrates on ends (justice, liberty, reconciliation, compassion or righteousness). The issue is not whether activities like soccer or flower shows are part of the program, but whether they are embraced in the mutual goals of the whole church or whether the church consists of people pursuing very different, separate goals.

The leadership of Jesus was clearly transformational, not transactional. In this story, Jesus and Peter did not trade with each other, but Peter joined Jesus to pursue Jesus' goal of fishing for men. Throughout the gospel stories this dynamic of transformational leadership can be observed. Jesus does not trade with his followers, but they join Jesus and adopt Jesus' goals as their own. Often Jesus' followers did not fully understand where Jesus was heading, and sometimes they got off track and had to be corrected by Jesus but the dominant dynamic was transformational not transactional.

Transformational leadership requires a high level of cooperation between leaders and followers. Unless people share the same goals as their leaders, transformational leadership cannot occur. Consequently leaders may sometimes desire transformational leadership but end up engaging in transactional leadership because followers don't share their goals. So while transformational leadership is more powerful, it may not be the fault of the leaders if it does not occur. In some contexts both transformational leadership and transactional leadership may occur concurrently. An example of this could be a chaplain in a state school (or some other secular environment). The chaplain may have a group of Christians who work closely with him or her and they share the same goals to follow Jesus and express the compassion of Jesus to others. The rest of the school would probably not share those particular goals but nevertheless see value in a chaplain. In these circumstances transformational leadership could be happening between the chaplain and the group of Christians while trans-actional leadership could occur between the chaplain and the broader school.

While leaders may not always have the level of cooperation nec-essary to achieve transformational leadership, many leaders make no attempt at transformational leadership even when it is within their reach. Transformational leadership, by definition, requires change and that means taking risks. Transactional leadership maintains the status quo and provides the most self-protection for the leaders themselves. If you don't rock the boat and keep everybody happy, you are more likely to win approval and keep your job. Transactional leaders often use the language of trans-formation and talk about how change is needed in our com-munities, churches and in ourselves, but no real effort is directed to those ends. It is not that they are necessarily hypocritical or insincere. Many would love to see those sorts of changes but the higher priority for them is keeping everybody happy and main-taining popularity. Transformational leadership requires courage and sacrifice. When ambition, power, self-protection or just com-fort and convenience dominate leaders, transactional leadership becomes the obvious choice. Jesus however was driven by higher motives.

Let's consider again the story of Beth at the beginning of this chapter. The fact that she was left to run the youth group on the day of her sister's funeral can be understood as simple thought-lessness. However that sort of thing is more likely to happen where transactional leadership is occurring. The church leaders didn't see themselves working together with Beth to achieve the same goals. In their minds Beth wanted to do youth ministry and they had generously given her the opportunity. It was a fair trade: Beth got what she wanted and the church leaders were able to fill the vacancy of the youth leader position. Beth should have felt honoured that they have given her this privilege. When this mindset is adopted, Beth's problems belong to Beth. The church leaders don't share Beth's goals so they are not likely to share her problems. If transformational leadership were occurring, the church leaders would see themselves working together with

Beth to achieve the same goals. Because they share the same goals, they would also share the same problems. They would be more likely to be aware of Beth's problems and more likely to respond to her needs.

Some claim that James Macgregor Burns' distinction between transactional leadership and transformational leadership is simply another way of distinguishing between management and leadership. What do you think?

Charismatic leadership

Charismatic leadership is a particular form of transformational leadership that is very powerful and can be either very good or very damaging. Max Weber defined charisma as 'a certain quality of an individual personality by virtue of which he is set apart from ordinary men and treated as endowed with supernatural, superhuman, or at least specifically exceptional qualities' [5].

In Luke's account of the call of Peter, Jesus possesses a charisma that is totally compatible with Weber's definition. In Mark's account the disciples responded simply to the call of Jesus. In Luke this response came only after the disciples realised that the divine was present. As in many other gospel stories, Jesus is presented as a character with exceptional or supernatural qualities.

The Jesus of the gospels bears a close resemblance to the descriptions of charismatic leaders in leadership literature. Robert Starratt [6] wrote that charismatic leaders are articulate and possess a clear understanding of themselves, their mission and context as well as passion, vision, powers of persuasion and courage. They have the capacity to connect with the values, meanings, identities and sense of purpose of their followers and in this lies their real power. A key characteristic is that charismatic leaders do not set out to lead but to achieve a goal. They would go alone if no one followed. They normally start with only a few followers who share their vision but eventually movements grow. Jay Conger.[7] described charismatic leaders as change agents with restless energy and dissatisfaction with the status quo. They are able to overcome problems and motivate people to change through clear, strategic vision. They are unconventional and have a tendency to overthrow traditions that stand in their way.

Charismatic leaders are both the breakers and maintainers of tradition. Edward Shils [8] takes Jesus' words, 'It is written, but I say unto you' as 'the characteristic expression of the charismatic'. Traditions are broken but they are also maintained and even renewed with new life and vitality. The tradition provides both an audience and a point of departure from which a new tradition emerges. In Jesus' own lifetime, Christianity was a sect of Judaism but it became much more and yet it retained its continuity with the Old Testament. Jesus challenged tradition and began a new tradition that maintained the relevance of the Old Testament.

All of the above qualities of charismatic leadership can be seen in Jesus in the gospel stories and many of them are evident in Luke's story of the call of Peter. The leadership of Jesus was both transformational and charismatic but charismatic leadership is fairly scarce and requires exceptional ability. There are many ways we can follow the example of Jesus in leadership but some things about Jesus are not transferable. Jesus had an understanding of human nature and could perform miracles and teach like no one else. He was the Son of God and as such, had unique charismatic qualities.

I suspect that most people who read this book will rarely, if ever, have the opportunity to exercise charismatic leadership. However as this book is about the leadership of Jesus, who was one of the great charismatic leaders, I have summarised some of the key characteristics of charismatic leadership so that we can appreciate this aspect of the leadership of Jesus. But we need to be aware that charismatic leadership is exceptional. Leaders like Billy Graham and Martin Luther King are fairly rare, with exceptional abilities and personalities. There is a lot we can learn from them but we need to recognise that charismatic leadership involves particular dynamics and relationships.

Transactional, transformational and charismatic leadership could all be seen as people-centred leadership. However in each of these types of leadership the relationships are quite different. In some cases, followers are trading with leaders, in others they are working together with leaders for change and in some cases they may be over-awed by their leaders. It is helpful to understand these different types of leadership and to be aware of the nature of our own leadership. Such awareness might help us to see better ways of going about leadership. It may also help leaders to understand the nature of their relationships with their follow-ers and what others might expect. Different types of leadership produce different kinds of relationships.

To lead means to influence people

Jesus worked hard to influence his followers. While Mark's story, in the previous chapter, emphasised the immediate, obedient response of the disciples, Luke's story describes the way Jesus influenced and persuaded them to make that response. Initially he involved Peter by asking for his help. Jesus borrowed Peter's boat. Secondly, Jesus communicated his values and beliefs. Peter was in the boat, presumably listening to the teaching of Jesus. Thirdly, Jesus helped Peter to catch fish. This was practical help and possibly very much needed because, up to that point, Peter had earned nothing that day from his fishing business. Fourthly, Jesus worked a miracle that demonstrated the presence of the divine. The way Jesus influenced them was tailor made to their lives. Jesus used fish and fishing to catch fishermen. He left the carpenter's shop, entered the fishermen's world and used what was meaningful to them to influence them for the kingdom.

Influence shapes the inner nature of people and helps them to really change, while force only produces outward compliance. Many of the Christian leaders who have made the most impact have had very little authority. How many people have had to obey Billy Graham or John Stott? Very few, but these men have influenced millions. For maximum impact, don't aim for power but aim for influence.

People respond to leaders who impart vision

Have you ever compared the vision statements of churches with what life is really like in those same churches? They usually express such wonderful aspirations about their relationships with God and/or their communities. In some cases you can sense a real, corporate effort to try to live up to the vision even though the church may fall short. In other cases you are left wondering how the vision statement has anything at all to do with the group of people who claim to own it. It came about because in a business meeting someone once composed a vision statement and everyone agreed that it was nice. The vision statement now hangs on the church wall and appears on some of the church's official documents, but it has very little to do with what really happens or even what people are trying to achieve. The church has no intention of being anything but the cosy club it has always been, but it likes to point to the vision hanging on the wall to explain its existence. Real vision gives power and direction to leadership while what is often called vision, is nothing more than an exercise of hypocrisy and denial. What can we learn about vision from Luke's story of the call of Peter?

Vision is future-oriented but it is built on the present. Jesus could see the Peter of the future, no longer catching fish but people. 'From now on you will catch men'. Jesus could see Peter the evangelist, pastor and church leader, yet he expressed that future vision in terms of Peter's present occupation of fishing. For vision to be effective it needs to see a better future emerging out of present conditions. Notice also that Jesus' vision is totally people-centred. It is not about numbers or buildings; it is about Peter. Jesus sees a different, future Peter, and he sees that a lot of other people will be different as a result of this. Imagine what the people you are working with could be like in five or ten year's time. What sort of people do you think God wants them to be? What will be their beliefs, values, attitudes, behaviours, skills and habits? What sorts of relationships will they have with each other and the broader community? What will need to happen to help them move from where they are now to this future vision? Vision requires realistic answers to these questions.

Vision is a key quality of leadership because it allows leaders to visualise a better future and inspires followers to new heights. When leaders have a vision for something better, they are able to readily identify what changes need to be made. Therefore vision is the engine-room of leadership. Values and beliefs encompassed in vision motivate the desire for change. Without a vision for something better, leadership cannot exist.

Vision does not come quickly or easily. It is not just a matter of writing a vision statement at a planning meeting. Real vision usually emerges slowly, grows over time, and develops out of deep-seated convictions and values. It is nurtured by Bible study, prayer, reading, experience, wrestling with tough issues, engaging your community and interaction with others. Vision needs to be stated in a way that captures the imagination of followers and it needs to be regularly restated or it becomes lost. The vision needs to shape the agenda and guide decisions. If it does not continually shape what happens or is easily forgotten, it is not real vision and is largely powerless.

Vision is essential to people-centred leadership. Vision is able to move people because it helps them to see a better future rising out of the present situation. For vision to be real it needs to emerge from who people are in the present and envisage what those same people can be in the future. Vision requires both honesty and faith. It involves being honest about who we are, yet willing to believe in what we can be.

How to nurture vision

(You can do this yourself, but it might be even better to discuss this with your leadership team or group.)

STEP 1 Dare to dream

Choose something you are involved in that is not as you think it should be. Choose something of substance that needs real, substantial change. For example, a group of people, your church, an organisation, your community, your nation.

Describe what you believe it should be like.

STEP 2 Identify the necessary changes

What are the changes that need to occur to move from the present situation to the future vision?

STEP 3 Dig beneath the surface

What beliefs and values lie behind the views you have expressed in steps 1 and 2 above? What is wrong with the way things are? Why are your suggested changes important? In what ways will people be better off?

The clearer your answers to these questions and the more effectively you are able communicate them, the more powerful will be your vision.

ENDNOTES

1. Morris, Leon, *The Gospel According to St. Luke An Introduction and Commentary,* Inter- Varsity Press, 1974, pp. 112.

2. Moloney, Francis J, *Disciples and Prophets,* Darton, Longman and Todd Ltd, 1980, pp. 138.

3. Morris, Leon, *The Gospel According to St. Luke An Introduction and Commentary,* Inter- Varsity Press, 1974, pp. 113.

4. Burns, James Macgregor , *Leadership,* Harper and Row, 1978, pp. 425ff.

5. Quoted by Starratt, Robert J, *The Drama of Leadership,* The Falmer Press, 1993, pp. 45.

6. Starratt, Robert J, *The Drama of Leadership,* The Falmer Press, 1993, pp. 44ff.

7. Conger, Jay A, *The Charismatic Leader,* Jossey-Bass Publishers, 1989.

8. Shils, Edward, *Tradition,* The University of Chicago Press, 1981, pp. 228ff.

Gary and Vicki's story

Gary and Vicki were active members of their community and their church. They had many friends in various community groups and often they took the opportunity to explain their Christian faith to these friends. Dozens had decided to become followers of Jesus over the years and Gary and Vicki invited them into their home for Bible study, prayer and support. It was all very exciting - that is, until they tried to introduce these people to their church.

Somehow these new Christians just did not fit in. They wanted to serve, have fellowship with other Christians, learn more from the Bible and participate in communion but they didn't like the way all these things were packaged in the church. They didn't like the music and so many of the practices seemed stale and formal. But it was the attitudes they encountered that presented the biggest problems. At one level most people were polite and welcoming, but at a deeper level, these new Christians were only tolerated and not really included. They noticed that if members of traditional church families had some problem or raised some matter of concern, they were given careful attention. In contrast, if Gary and Vicki's friends raised concerns, they would be given brief attention, but then quickly disregarded. The impression conveyed to them was that they didn't really matter because they didn't have a pedigree.

Most of Gary and Vicki's friends came to church for at least a few months and some persevered for a few years. They hoped that acceptance would come with time, but in the end it became obvious that they would never be accepted. Eventually every one of these people left that church, except for one lady who had married one of the men from the church. Most moved on to other churches, while a few dropped out of the Christian scene all together. The irony was that this church regularly organised evangelistic outreaches and invited people to come to Christ and come to church. Yet sadly, if anybody ever responded, they would never be accepted.

Gary and Vicki went to see Lloyd, who was a highly respected member of the church board. They expressed their joy that their friends had come to know Jesus and had found homes in other churches, but they also shared their frustration that they had not been able to find a home in their own church. Gary and Vicki were not sure that they could stay in that church, since they were no longer confident that it was a church where they could bring their friends. They faced a choice between loyalty to their church and their desire to win and disciple new Christians. Lloyd was sympathetic and expressed his disappointment at the way things had turned out. However he also defended the attitudes of the church. 'This is *our* church', Lloyd said politely. 'If they want to come to our church, they must fit in with us. It's up to them to adjust to us. We don't have to make any changes for them.' Gary and Vicki did not expect that the church should change every-thing for their friends. There are lots of opinions about service styles and music, and you can't please everyone. However the church was willing to compromise and negotiate with people from established church families, while the concerns of Gary and Vicki's friends were just dismissed automatically. It seemed that the church was a club and you could only be a full member if you came from the right background.

This story is not unusual. There have been many keen Christians who wanted to show the love of Christ in their community and were disappointed to find that it was a church that let them down. This is often discussed as a problem to do with music and worship styles. Those issues are very real and relevant but the real problem goes far deeper. It is fundamentally an issue of values and which values have the highest priority. For some churches, maintaining the comfortable club with all its traditions and keeping the long-standing members happy, is of far more value than the extension of God's kingdom. To them, there are only a few people who really matter; there is little concern for anyone else.

When people feel valued, they are more likely to be able to work things out. When evangelism, discipleship, social concern and justice are valued above the comforts of the church club, individual preferences are more likely to give way to these higher values. Leaders with clear values have a firm basis for making decisions. They know why they do the things they do and they are not merely at the mercy of anyone who can mount political pressure. Clear values help to sort out priorities, but they also increase the likelihood of conflict.

The story of the call of Levi

Once again Jesus went out beside the lake. A large crowd came to him, and he began to teach them. As he walked along, he saw Levi son of Alphaeus sitting at the tax collector's booth. 'Follow me,' Jesus told him, and Levi got up and followed him.

While Jesus was having dinner at Levi's house, many tax collectors and 'sinners' were eating with him and his disciples, for there were many who followed him. When the teachers of the law who were Pharisees saw him eating with the 'sinners' and tax collectors, they asked his disciples: 'Why does he eat with tax collector's and sinners?'

On hearing this, Jesus said to them, 'It is not the healthy who need a doctor, but the sick. I have not come to call the righteous, but sinners.' Mark 2:13-17

Have you ever been accused of being in bad company? Have you ever been caught mixing with the wrong crowd? If so, you are in good company, because Jesus got in trouble for that. Jesus in bad company! For many, that sounds like a contradiction, but Jesus said that being in bad company was at the very core of his mission. Who is this person who is considered to be such bad company for Jesus? His name is Levi and he is also called Matthew. Years later, he would write Matthew's Gospel, but it created quite a stir when Jesus first called Levi to be one of his disciples. The story of the call of Levi provides a window into the leadership values of Jesus.

This story has much in common with the story of the call of Peter, Andrew, James and John, explored in Chapter 2. The setting is again by a lake. Once again the initiative is with Jesus, who meets Levi at his place of business and calls him to follow. Once again there is the immediate, wordless and uncompromising response. Again, it is a costly response as Levi leaves his profitable business to follow Jesus.[1] There is though, a big difference between these two stories and it involves the social setting. The fishermen were involved in a respectable occupation while Levi was a tax collector and was therefore, an outcast. Tax collectors were agents for the Roman oppressors; not the Jewish government and they were hated as Lane explains: [2]

> Such officials were detested everywhere and were classed with the vilest of men. The practice of leasing the customs duty of a district at a fixed sum encouraged gross oppression by tax officers anxious to secure as large a profit as possible. When a Jew entered the customs service he was regarded as an outcast from society: he was disqualified as a judge or a witness in a court session, was excommunicated from the synagogue and in the eyes of the community his disgrace extended to his family.

The point of this story is that while discipleship is costly, it is not exclusive. Even an outcast like Levi is welcome to become a follower of Jesus.

As a spontaneous expression of gratitude, Levi hosts a banquet for Jesus, which is also attended by Jesus' disciples and 'many tax collectors and 'sinners'. The word 'sinners' is not used here in a theological sense, whereby we are all sinners because we have done wrong. Here 'sinners' refers to a social group who did not live up to the standards imposed by the Pharisees. The Pharisees believed that such people should be avoided, but Jesus is not only associating with these people, he is partying with them. On seeing this, the Pharisees ask, 'Why does he eat with tax collectors and sinners?' This is not an honest question, but a complaint (see Luke 5:30). They are implying that Jesus should not mix with such people. He had no right to be in bad company.

The Pharisees thought that they had found a major flaw in Jesus. They had caught him in the act too. How could Jesus deny it? What excuses could he offer? In response, Jesus makes no excuses but affirms that this is the whole purpose of his coming. He has come to have relationships with sinners like these. Jesus replies, 'It is not the healthy who need a doctor, but the sick.' He argues that if these people are as sick as the Pharisees claim, then they need a doctor. Based on their own diagnosis of these people as morally sick, this is logic the Pharisees could not deny.

Jesus further clarifies the purpose of his coming: 'I have not come to call the righteous but sinners'. Because the Pharisees are so confident of their own righteousness, they can't recognise that they too are sinners and they see no need to respond to the call of repentance. Only sinners can hear Jesus' call to repentance. The Pharisees won't mix with sinners because they believe that there is a great gap between themselves and such people. Indeed, a great gap does exist, but it is not a gap between one person and another. It is a gap between *all* people and God. The irony is that while the Pharisees are reinforcing an artificial gap, in this very story Jesus had eliminated the real gap: the Son of God is sitting and eating with sinners.

This story reinforces the point of the preceding story in Mark's gospel verse 10, 'that the Son of Man has authority on earth to forgive sins'. That story is about the paralysed man who was lowered through the roof of a house to be healed and Jesus said to him, 'Your sins are forgiven'. Having told that story, Mark now tells the story of the call of Levi to show that, because Jesus has the authority to forgive sins, he has bridged the gap between God and sinners. The Son of God is eating with sinners like Levi and his friends: traitors, cheats and social outcasts. The whole incident emphasises grace and anticipates the end of history when Jesus will feast with sinners in the kingdom of God.

A number of aspects of value-based leadership can be observed in this story.

Jesus displayed inclusiveness as a key value

Leadership is essentially about values and inclusiveness was one of the key values of Jesus. Anyone was welcome to become a follower of Jesus, no matter who they were or what they had done. In contrast to the exclusive attitudes of the Pharisees, the inclusiveness of Jesus is remarkable. Jesus did not just include Levi the tax collector as one of his disciples but he also included a Zealot, a member of a group that actively opposed Roman occupation and paying taxes to Rome. Jesus served the sick, disabled and lepers as well as male and female, poor and rich, and Jews and Gentiles. Everyone was welcome but not everyone was willing to follow Jesus.

This story teaches two things about being a Christian. Firstly, it is conditional. Levi had to respond to the call of Jesus in order to become one of Jesus' followers. He had to repent and enter into a relationship with Jesus. There are conditions to being a Christian. We can only become Christians if we repent and follow Jesus.

Secondly, it is unmerited. No one is a Christian because they measure up to God's standards. No one deserves to be accepted into God's family. Jesus accepted Levi in spite of his obvious failures. Discipleship is costly, but it is not exclusive, rather it is inclusive. While inclusion within the community of Jesus is conditional on following Jesus, it is unmerited. Jesus is willing to accept anyone, no matter who they are, or what they have done.

Leadership must epitomise grace or it falls short of the leadership of Jesus. Any attempt to restrict membership on the basis of superiority due to social class, moral history and the like, is a denial of the grace of God. Leaders' attitudes must be characterised by a willingness to include. This was one of the values that separated the leadership of Jesus from that of the Pharisees. The Pharisees would not accept Levi and his friends because they did not measure up to their standards or fit into their group. For ministry to be Christian we must welcome and seek out all kinds of people. Followers of Jesus must be concerned for all types of people: the outcast as well as the respectable, the sick as well as the healthy, the disabled as well as the athletic, the unpopular as well as the popular and the poor as well as the rich.

There are many Christian groups that practice inclusion and welcome all kinds of people into their fellowship. On the other hand the experience of Gary and Vicki in the introduction to this chapter is all too common. In this subtle kind of exclusion, no one would tell anyone to go away and most would smile and be polite. Everyone is welcome to attend, but not everyone will be accepted into the group. It is only the people from the in-group who matter and only their concerns, suggestions and ideas will be considered. Exclusive attitudes don't just happen by accident; they have a purpose. The purpose is to keep 'inferior' people in their place. They also allow the people in control to exclude those who might threaten to take over their positions or introduce new ideas.

The groups that practice exclusive attitudes like those encountered by Gary and Vicki often deny it. The church or group pretends to welcome everybody while subtle undercurrents present a very different picture. Sometimes however, Christian leaders intentionally embrace exclusive strategies and teach that the way to achieve results is to include certain people and effectively exclude the rest. Here are two examples of this sort of teaching.

The 20/80 Principle[3]

The 20/80 principle teaches that leaders should focus on the people who will be of most use to them and not give much time to the rest. Leaders are taught to identify the people who are most capable of helping them (or hurting them if they get off side). Usually these people would make up no more than 20% of their following. Leaders are then taught that 80% of their time and effort should be spent on those 20%. Clearly, unless people are seen as either a major asset or a major potential threat, they are counted as not worthy of quality time and effort.

This approach stands in total contrast to the example of Jesus who spent so much time with outcasts, lepers, women, the poor and the sick. Jesus gave considerable personal time to such people and did not merely delegate their care to others, as if they were below him. To imagine that the Jesus of the Gospels dealt with people by calculating who was likely to provide the best return is sheer fantasy. This approach also contrasts with Jesus' teaching on servant leadership, 'whoever wants to be great among you must be your servant, and whoever wants to be first must be slave of all'.[4] According to Jesus, Christian leadership is about serving others. To follow Jesus means that we must reject strategies that concentrate on those most able to serve us. This is not to say that identifying and training future leadership is not valid. Leadership development is essential if followers of Jesus are to address the needs of the many different people in our world. Spending quality time with people in key roles is also important. These are things that Jesus did, but he did them in the context of an inclusive ministry. Jesus gave considerable time to developing future leaders, but he spent a lot of time on other people as well. Leadership modelled on Jesus serves others, and equips others to serve others. It is not an exercise in identifying those most able to serve us at the exclusion of others.

The Homogeneous Unit Principle

Some church growth theorists have strongly promoted the Homogeneous Unit Principle (HUP). The theory is that people like to mix with other people similar to themselves, and church congregations will grow faster if this is observed. We are told that some churches should be formed specifically for business people who should reach other business people. Other churches can focus on professional people who will be better equipped to reach other professionals and so on. Pastors are even taught to form a profile of the sort of person they want in their church and then to aim specifically for that sort of person. For example, a church might aim for tertiary-educated, professionals between thirty and forty years of age, conservative voters, married with children. They aim for that sort of person and little or no effort is directed at other people who fall outside the profile.

John had schizophrenia and he started to attend a church that adopted the HUP and targeted professional people. After a few weeks the pastor phoned Hugh, who organised a Christian community outreach that ministered to a range of people, some of them with mental illnesses. The pastor asked Hugh if he would be prepared to take John into his fellowship, claiming that his church did not know how to help John. Hugh replied, 'We will take John if you don't want him, but your church probably has more doctors and medical professionals than any other church in this city. Your fellowship is better equipped to help John than almost anybody else. Have you not thought that God may have sent him to you so that you might consider how you could help him?' What was the real reason behind this desire to refer John to another group? Was it really about the church's capacity to help John? Or was it that John was simply not the sort of person they really wanted at their church?

What might have happened if Jesus had adopted the HUP? Jesus first called Peter, Andrew, James and John, Galilean fishermen, probably in their twenties. Imagine them discussing others who might be included in their group. They won't aim for Levi: a tax collector, outcast and friend of the Romans. People won't feel comfortable if he is in the group. Simon the Zealot would be too radical and political and Nicodemus the Pharisee is far too stuffy and threatening. They should not waste their time either with any Samaritan women who just might hang around wells, nor with Roman centurions because some people feel threatened by other races. Who would feel comfortable sharing communion with lepers? Avoid the lepers and also the poor. They must focus on people that make fishermen feel comfortable.

There is a place for homogeneous units in Christian ministry. For example, people who attempt to minister to youth, students, athletes or housewives are often engaging with groups that are homogeneous. It would be foolish to neglect opportunities that arise with groups that are fairly homogeneous. Homogeneous units often provide a means to an end, but they must never become ends in themselves. As these people choose to follow Jesus, hopefully they will be embraced within a broader body of believers where they will experience unity with people who are different from themselves. In the body of Christ 'there is neither Jew nor Greek, slave nor free, male or female, for you are all one in Christ Jesus'.[5] The New Testament envisages people ultimately being embraced into inclusive, yet diverse fellowships, where slave and free, rich and poor, worship and serve together in the Body of Christ.

Christians grow when they mix with people who are different from themselves. These growth experiences are often uncomfortable because they challenge our prejudices and push us out of our comfort zones. The HUP robs Christians of this growth. It protects their comfort zones and ensures that their prejudices can never be disturbed. Indeed, it can be hard to accept and serve people who are different, but this is simply part of the cost of discipleship. To follow Jesus means to embrace inclusiveness so that even outcasts and traitors like Levi are made welcome.

Jesus displayed identification as a key value

In this story Jesus was eating with outcasts and in doing so, he presents for all leaders a model of identification. There was no sense of superiority with Jesus. We see him eating with Levi and his friends and mixing with them on their level. Jesus did not erect any social barriers. He operated on the same social level as ordinary people. Furthermore, this is not an isolated incident, but typical of Jesus' life. He was humble, accessible and approachable. Though Jesus was the Son of God, he identified with his followers and operated on their social level.

Not all Christian leaders follow Jesus' example. Some go to great lengths to separate themselves from others and try to appear superior. Some believe that leaders should have higher incomes, better houses and luxury cars to demonstrate their superiority. Some restrict access to themselves to create an impression that they are separate from ordinary people. In some churches it is very difficult for ordinary people to see the pastor. Access to busy people does need to be carefully controlled. Christian leaders have a lot of responsibilities and can't be available to everyone, all of the time. However, the devices that are used to restrict access to leaders sometimes have more to do with ensuring people know their place, than about time management. Restricting access to leaders can be part of creating a persona to give the impression that leaders are so special, that they are beyond ordinary people. It can be part of a pretence that their work is so important that the issues affecting their followers are not worthy of their time.

Leaders should renounce these devices and learn to 'do nothing out of selfish ambition or vain conceit, but in humility consider others better than yourselves'.[6] That passage goes on to describe how the leadership of Jesus was distinguished by servanthood, humility and identification with human beings, not by superiority and separation.

Christian symbols should connect with the values of Jesus

'Now let us all prepare ourselves to take communion', says Pastor Ron as he stands behind a small table, covered by a crisp, white table cloth, on which the bread and wine has been carefully placed. 'This is the way that Jesus has asked us to remember him and before we take part, it is important that we prepare our hearts. Let's pause for a moment to confess our sin and seek the Lord's forgiveness. *(pause)* This bread represents the body of Jesus that was broken for us and the wine represents his blood. Before we share these symbols, let us reflect on the sacrifice Jesus made for us at Calvary. As we partake of this together in a few minutes, let us sincerely thank the Lord for his mercy, grace and forgiveness. Now, hear what Paul wrote in 1 Corinthians 11, "The Lord Jesus, on the night he was betrayed, took bread, and ...".' And so the communion service proceeds, reverently and thoughtfully remembering what Jesus has done for us.

What could possibly be wrong with this? If we put aside the debates about the proper theology and practice of communion, what could be wrong when Christians are sincerely and reverently celebrating communion? The story of the call of Levi suggests that there could be plenty wrong. This sort of thing could even be something that God actually hates. It is not just about how sincere or thankful we are when we take communion. It is about whether we embrace grace, mercy and forgiveness in the way we treat others. Do we merely thank God for his grace and mercy, and then keep it to ourselves, or do we pass on that grace, mercy and forgiveness to others? In our daily lives, do we really connect with the values that lie behind the symbols of the bread and wine? Let's come back to what Jesus said to the Pharisees.

Jesus told the Pharisees that they had lost touch with the meaning of the religion they practiced. Matthew's account of this incident (Matthew 9:9-13) contains a sentence that is not in Mark's gospel. In verse 13, Matthew adds to Jesus' reply to the Pharisees, 'But go and learn what this means: "I desire mercy, not sacrifice"'. This is a quote from Hosea 6:6 where the Israelites are condemned for their lack of compassion and justice towards their fellow man while persisting in the ritual temple sacrifices. Jesus points out that the Pharisees had not learnt from Hosea. By quoting 'I desire mercy, not sacrifice', Jesus was rebuking the Pharisees for caring greatly for the mechanics and rituals of religion while denying the substantive values that lie behind them, values like justice, mercy and compassion. Hosea was saying that God doesn't want their sacrifices if they are not going to treat others with mercy and compassion. Jesus was pointing out that the attitude of the Pharisees to Levi and his friends showed that they did not understand what the sacrifices meant. The sacrifices of Judaism were symbols of the grace, mercy and compassion of God. The Pharisees affirmed the symbols while denying their meaning in the way they lived. When they offered sacrifices, they embraced and celebrated the mercy of God, yet they had no mercy on others. For Jesus, religious symbols were not ends in themselves but statements of meaning that had to be lived out.

In this story, Jesus reconnected the symbol to the meaning. Modern Christians also have symbols, like communion and baptism. These rituals of the Christian faith are statements of the grace and mercy of God. When we take the bread and wine of communion, we celebrate God's mercy and compassion. It is not enough to thank God that he has treated us with love, mercy and forgiveness. We must extend mercy and forgiveness to others. If we practice communion yet fail to be merciful and forgiving, we have disconnected the symbols from their meaning. The bread and wine must remind us, that as God has shown mercy to us, we *must* show mercy to others. How can we celebrate the sacrifice and compassion of Christ, and not be committed to a life of compassion and sacrifice ourselves?

For many Christians and their leaders, what really matters is not values like mercy and compassion, but meetings where we celebrate communion, sing hymns and listen to sermons. As long as people come, the programs run smoothly and the budgets are balanced, that's all that really matters. In response, Jesus said, 'I desire mercy, not sacrifice'. God wants us to truly embrace mercy, not just the religious symbols of mercy. Christian leaders need to be careful not to get so caught up with meetings and programs, that they lose touch with the reality that lies behind it all and fail to be people who live out mercy and compassion. Leaders who practice the Christian symbols yet fail to uphold and teach mercy and compassion, have lost contact with the very meaning of those symbols. Jesus' values of mercy, compassion and justice are central to the exercise of Christian leadership. Don't just practice Christian symbols; strive to reconnect people with what those symbols mean.

Some values should have a higher priority

When Jesus said, 'I desire mercy, not sacrifice', he did not mean that mercy is good while sacrifices are bad. Both are good, but mercy is more important than religious rituals and traditions. This is not a rejection of sacrifices by Jesus, but a statement of priorities. Jesus was not dismissing the rituals of Judaism as unimportant, rather he was signalling that other values were more important. Jesus valued the temple, sacrifices and scriptures of Israel. It is because he valued them that he protested against the abuse of these traditions. Religious traditions and symbols were important to Jesus, but compassion, mercy and mission were more important. Many values are good, but some should have priority.

Jesus demonstrated in this story a clear hierarchy of values. James MacGregor Burns affirmed the need to establish a hierarchy of values, with the more important values identified and given priority. He claimed that leaders who say they embrace many values without establishing such a hierarchy are not acting as leaders at all, but merely 'seeking the widest possible consensus on the basis of the thinnest - or least thoughtful - consensus'.[7] Political leaders have to think clearly about this issue. National security, prosperity, individual liberty, equality, justice and compassion are values that most communities would embrace. However it is the values that are given the highest priority which will determine the social climate of those communities. Communities that put prosperity and individual liberty on top of the hierarchy will be substantially different from those that give priority to justice and equality. It is not that the other values are totally rejected, but that the values at the top of the hierarchy call the tune. Some recent political debates in Australia and other western countries boil down to whether national security or national prosperity should be elevated above such things as justice in our hierarchy of values.

It is of vital importance for Christian leaders to be clear about the values that should have priority. Most churches and Christian organisations would claim to value things like compassion, mission, fellowship, tradition and harmony. So they should, because these are all good things. The difference is not in which values are included in the list, but which values are put at the top of the list. It is the values that are given priority that call the tune for the whole group. The story of the call of Levi makes it clear that Jesus gave priority to mercy, compassion and mission and these values were considered to be far more important than tradition, religious rituals and harmony.

Many churches and Christian groups have the opposite priorities to Jesus. No one in them would say that mission and compassion are not important but when it comes to the crunch, tradition, harmony and comfort always win. There may be lots of talk about evangelism, doing works of compassion and involvement in mission, but these will only be allowed when people don't have to change anything or make any sacrifices or where they can be embraced without any likelihood of conflict. That way Christians play lip service to compassion and mission, but then ensure that it is always squashed. It is the values at the top of the hierarchy that determine whether Christian groups engage in the mission of Jesus or are just religious social clubs. Mercy, compassion and mission suffocate when tradition and harmony play the tune. On the other hand, tradition and fellowship are enriched when mission and compassion are at the top of the priorities. The Pharisees gave tradition and group acceptance top priority and were a miserable lot. Jesus gave top priority to mercy, compassion and mission yet led a wonderful fellowship that brought new life into the tired old traditions of Judaism.

I asked several Christian leaders which values they place at the top of their hierarchy of values. One leader said that he was intentional about allowing the teaching of the Bible to over-ride organisational considerations. For example, he believes that wealthy donors should be treated the same as all other donors. If doing what the Bible says, means that the organisation will make less money or be less popular, then so be it. Another man quoted 1 Corinthians 13:13, 'the greatest of these is love'. For him, love is the top value and the social expression of love is justice. He also pointed to the fruit of the Spirit: 'love, joy, peace, patience, kindness, gentleness and self-control' listed in Galatians 5: 22-23. The evidence of these provides for him a clear indicator of whether his leadership reflects the spirit of the gospel.

A third leader always asks two questions. First: how does this affect people? Second: what does this mean in kingdom terms? That is, what does this mean for the total work of God, not just his own church or organisation? Another leader identified servant leadership as his highest value because Jesus specifically commanded it. Second comes integrity and honesty because, if Christianity is the truth, truth cannot be compromised. His third highest value is that everyone is important. Everyone is part of the Body of Christ, so that even the most broken and vulnerable must be included or the body is denied.

All the above leaders measured their priorities against the teaching of the Bible. They may have focused on different texts or doctrines, but they looked to the Bible to establish which values should have priority.

Leaders must not only have clear priorities themselves but must help their followers sort out their own hierarchy of values. One of the disturbing things to come out of the genocide that occurred in Rwanda during 1994 was the large number of active Christians that joined in the killings. (There were also many Rwandan Christians who did not participate in killings.) There had been a revival in Rwanda and many had become Christians. However when the tribal warfare started Christians from both the Hutu and Tutsi tribes joined in the killing and even killed their brothers and sisters in Christ. Where did their true priorities lie? In church they affirmed that Jesus is Lord, yet when the pressure was on, loyalty to the tribe had priority over loyalty to Jesus.

I am concerned by the priorities I observe in some active Australian Christians. For many, it seems that maintaining a comfortable, materialistic lifestyle is top priority and the demands of Christian discipleship come well down the list. The priority is houses, cars, possessions, holidays and pleasure while ensuring that church membership and daily quiet times are maintained. I wonder how many Christians allow themselves to be informed by the teaching of the Bible when they consider how to respond to social issues. For example, when faced with the temptation of racism, how many stop to think that Jesus was not European and that he treated people of other races with respect? Do we allow our attitudes to be informed by what the Bible teaches about foreigners and refugees? Do we stop to consider that Jesus, Paul, Moses, David and the whole nation of Israel were refugees? When considering when to support war, do we weigh up what Jesus said about revenge and loving our enemies? Do we really wrestle with what the Bible teaches or do our political loyalties take priority over our loyalty to Jesus, his teaching and example?

Maintaining the values of Jesus was a continual battle for the apostles. The New Testament writings reflect an ongoing struggle to bring Christians back to the key doctrines and values of

Jesus. The various epistles were written so that churches would not slide into conforming to the wishes of their members and the prevailing wisdom of the day. The epistles correct the drift and bring their readers back to Jesus. Contemporary Christian leaders may well ask if they would be prepared to fight the sorts of battles that Paul, Peter and John fought. Are they more concerned with maintaining the image, traditions and comfort zones of their churches and organisations? It is not enough to identify a list of values. Which values are given priority? Which values are placed at the top of the hierarchy? What needs to change?

The values of Jesus lead to conflict

The gospel narratives record that Jesus' ministry involved conflict In this story, Jesus is in conflict with the Pharisees, who opposed him because of his acceptance of Levi and his friends. The story immediately before this one involves conflict between the teachers of the Law and Jesus, because of his claim to be able to forgive sins (Mark 2:5-7). The story that follows involves a significant difference if not conflict, with the disciples of John the Baptist (Mark 2:18-22). As the gospels unfold, the conflict with the Pharisees and other religious leaders grows to the point where Jesus is murdered. All through his ministry, Jesus encountered conflict.

Some people seem to believe that all conflicts are wrong or at least represent failures of leadership. They think that Christians should always get along with others and not have major differences with them. That view does not fit with Jesus or any other major leader in the Bible. Moses, David, Elijah, Nehemiah, Jeremiah, Paul and many others experienced continual and sometimes extreme conflict. Great leadership is forged in the furnace of conflict. Another common misconception is that leadership equals popularity. The truth is that genuine leaders are both loved and hated. Leaders not only have followers, they usually also have opponents, even enemies. Leaders have strongly held values and beliefs, and they fight for them. Whether or not you like particular leaders, will largely depend on whether you agree with them.

James MacGregor Burns[8] wrote that conflict is an inevitable part of genuine leadership. Real leadership challenges morals and values, seeks real change and allows people to make choices between real alternatives. 'Leaders ... do not shun conflict; they confront it, exploit it, ultimately embody it'.[9] It is in the environment of conflict that leaders often emerge and it is leaders who often create conflict. Jay Conger[10] wrote that charismatic leaders in particular, tend to create conflict because of the way they threaten and reshape tradition. The guardians of these traditions tend to mobilise themselves in opposition. That is one reason why the Pharisees and other Jewish religious leaders were so opposed to Jesus. They knew that he wanted change and they were intent on keeping their traditions untouched.

Conflict is not only inevitable; it is often necessary. Total harmony is not a sign of good leadership, but of the lack of leadership. It may mean that no one is standing for the values of Jesus and that everyone is drifting with the status quo of a comfortable club. It may mean that the group is exclusive and only includes people with similar ideas and values. Such groups are often very peaceful but this is not necessarily because they are good at managing conflict. They are often completely unable to handle conflict and avoid conflict by excluding anyone who might present a challenge. 'Leaders' that set a pattern of avoiding conflict may pay a heavy price. Due to cowardliness, they may well fail to 'fight the good fight of faith'[11]. If we don't stand for the values of Jesus, our activity cannot be called 'Christian leadership', and one day we will have to give an account of our service.

At a practical level, churches and Christian groups benefit from a healthy level of conflict. Environments where people can debate and critique beliefs, programs and practices encourage clearer thinking and the development of improved programs. When someone says 'I don't agree with ...' or 'I think we could do a lot better at ...', conflicts often follow. Yet if those conflicts are managed well, they can lead to vast improvements. Discussions like these are uncomfortable, but if we avoid the discomfort, we lose the benefits of new insights, opportunities and innovations.

Genuine leaders don't avoid conflict. However conflict does need to be managed. Conflict can be functional, but also be very dysfunctional. There are both healthy and very damaging ways to deal with conflict.

Some key ideas for managing conflict

Be assertive, not aggressive

Aggressive behaviour attacks other people, while assertion communicates your concerns and perhaps requests a different course of action. If you are deeply troubled by something and do nothing about it (non-assertion), the problem will probably be prolonged and often becomes worse. Serious problems rarely go away by themselves.

Don't allow yourself to merely react

Think carefully about how you should respond to conflict situations. Rather than just reacting, consider what you should do and how you should do it. Also think about the best time to respond, but don't put it off indefinitely.

Use language that states your concerns rather than attacks other people

For example, 'I'm not sure I understood what you were trying to say and found it confusing. Could we talk more about this?' is far better than 'You are a hopeless communicator. As usual, everything you said was completely stupid.'

Think about what you are trying to achieve in the conflict

Often our natural reaction in conflict is to seek a win-lose solution, that is, we want to win and make the other people lose. For example, 'We are only going to play the music I like, not that rubbish you want us to have.' Sometimes people settle for a lose-win. They back off when they see conflict looming, even if their concerns are valid.

For example, 'I know lots of people who agree with me, but I can't be bothered making an issue out of it.' Usually it is best to strive for a win-win solution where you try to address the key concerns of all the parties. For example, 'I would love to sit down and talk, to see if we can discover some way to embrace everyone's concerns about the music.' Often a win-win solution is not possible, but in serious conflicts, it is worth the effort to try.

Listen first

'Everyone should be quick to listen, slow to speak and slow to become angry.'[12] Often we do exactly the opposite: we are quick to become angry, quick to speak and very slow to listen. It is easy to construct an idea in our minds which we think represents what the other person is saying and refuse to stop, listen and really understand. We must have an openness to hear the other person's point of view.

Speak the truth in love

Twisting the truth is easy in conflict situations and it is easy to forget about 'speaking the truth in love.'[13] That doesn't just mean telling the truth, but also loving the other people in how we handle the truth.

Treat people with humility and respect

'Do nothing out of selfish ambition or vain conceit, but in humility consider others better than yourselves.'[14] Humility does not mean to put yourself down, but to elevate others. These attitudes do not guarantee that you will be successful in getting what you want, but you will

> maintain your integrity and are more likely to deal with people in ways that please God.
>
> Christian leaders should always strive for Christ-like attitudes in any conflict situation.

Many conflicts can be resolved, but the life of Jesus demonstrates that some conflicts cannot be resolved. Jesus could never achieve his mission and resolve the conflict with the Pharisees. As long as Jesus claimed to be able to forgive sins, as long as he cared for marginalised people like Levi, and objected to injustice and the misuse of the Old Testament, he would always be a target for the Pharisees. To resolve that conflict Jesus would have had to cease being the Son of God. At times Jesus escalated the conflict with the Pharisees and religious leaders. It is hard to imagine that Jesus was trying to resolve conflict while he was cleansing the temple.

If we follow Jesus, conflict is unavoidable. We should not seek conflict, rather we should seek to embrace the mission and values of Jesus, making mercy, compassion, justice and reconciliation our priorities. In doing that we should seek peace, but not be surprised if we encounter conflict. Like Jesus, when we encounter conflict, we must not let it deter us from the mission and values that drive us.

ENDNOTES

1. Molony, Francis J, *Disciples and Prophets,* Darton, Longman and Todd Ltd, 1980, pp. 137.

2. Lane, William L, *The Gospel According to Mark,* Williams B. Eerdmans Publishing Company, 1974, pp. 101.

3. An example of this teaching is found in *Developing the Leader Within You* by John C. Maxwell, Thomas Nelson Publishers, 1993 pp. 21ff.

4. Mark 10:43-44

5. Galatians 3:28

6. Philippians 2:3

7.Burns, James MacGregor, *Leadership,* Harper and Row, 1978, pp. 432.

8. Burns, James MacGregor, *Leadership,* Harper and Row, 1978, pp. 36-41,453-454.

9. Burns, James MacGregor, *Leadership,* Harper and Row, 1978, pp. 39.

10. Conger, Jay A, *The Charismatic Leader,* Jossey-Bass Publishers, 1989, pp. 5-8.

11. 1 Timothy 6:12

12. James 1:19

13. Ephesians 4:15

14. Philippians 2:3

Ken's story

Ken was a good man, sincere Christian and a preacher who could
inspire people to follow Jesus, but it was a big mistake to make
him the chief executive officer of a Christian organisation. One of
his strengths was his creativity and he was continually coming up
with new ideas. Ken could talk up these ideas too, and initially
get staff, volunteers and donors really motivated and excited. He
was big on vision, big on promises, but consistently failed to follow through on the detail. Ken was good at doing things himself,
and he could tell others *what* to do, but he could not tell others
how to do it. He was totally unable to empower his team.

Ken's record on team leadership was a litany of errors. He would
send staff on assignments and tell them that all the arrangements had been made, but they would arrive to find that no one
was expecting them. Staff members were regularly assigned to
tasks only to find that money and other promised resources were
lacking. This was very frustrating and eventually Ken lost all trust
and credibility. The staff found that many of the things that Ken
said turned out to be untrue. It was not that he deliberately tried
to deceive them, but more wishful thinking that all would be
well. He was so impatient to proceed with ideas that he would
go ahead and hope for the best, rather than plan and prepare.

Ken saw everyone else as a rival and he had to ensure that they
were kept in their place so as not to threaten his position. Only
his ideas were ever accepted and he always had to appear to be
the leader and organiser. Ken trusted no one else with any of
the tasks of senior leadership and knowledge of the organisation was kept to himself, so that staff would not know what was
happening. Ken would try to create an impression of influence
and importance by dropping the names of politicians and other
important people. He would also talk big to the broader community and promise things that the staff and organisation simply

could not deliver.

Ken provided no training for his staff and starved them of funding, resources and information. He only delegated responsibilities that kept people in minor roles. Ken saw no need to appoint a second-in-command and he never made use of planning teams because he decided everything and presented his plans as a *fait accompli*. It was difficult for staff to grow and to develop. They ended up as isolated individuals, each doing their own tasks, with no sense of coordination, unity or team. They were lonely and disheartened and, when they encountered problems, they received no backing or support from Ken. Whenever staff failed, Ken left them to take the consequences alone and did not take these as opportunities to help staff reflect and learn from their mistakes.

Eventually, Ken was asked for his resignation. He had been the chief executive officer of that organisation for eight years and in that time, it had declined from twelve staff to two, and its operational branches had been reduced from nine to one. Almost all the financial supporters of the organisation had been lost and they had to start again. The man who took over from Ken faced a very difficult task to rebuild the organisation, as no one had been prepared for senior leadership and no one really knew the true state of affairs.

There is an enormous difference between doing Christian ministry yourself and leading a team. No matter how capable an individual might be, there is always a limit to what one person can do and eventually the work of one person must come to an end. A team expands the work, not only by increasing the number of workers, but each new person adds new abilities, knowledge and wisdom that can be tapped for the common good. While one person can only be in one place at a time, the members of a team can be in many places at once and teams are able to continue well after the founding members have moved on.

Imagine what would have happened if Jesus had not recruited a team to expand and carry on the work. Jesus did an immense amount of good, but without the team, the whole movement would have ended at the Ascension, when he left this earth to return to his Father. If it were not for that team of disciples, none of the events recorded in the Acts of the Apostles would have occurred and Christianity as we know it would not have survived to this day. The fact that the Christian church could expand so rapidly after his death is a testament to how well Jesus formed, trained and equipped his ministry team. So far this book has considered how Jesus recruited individuals to be his followers. This chapter explores how Jesus formed these men, as well as other followers into a ministry team. Jesus has much to teach us about team focus, expectations, structure, spirituality, training and responding to failure.

The story of the appointing of the twelve apostles

Jesus went up into the hills and called to him those he wanted, and they came to him. He appointed twelve - designating them apostles - that they might be with him and that he might send them out to preach and to have authority to drive out demons. These are the twelve he appointed: Simon (to whom he gave the name Peter); James son of Zebedee, and his brother John (to them he gave the name Boanerges, which means Sons of Thunder); Andrew, Philip, Bartholomew, Matthew, Thomas, James son of Alphaeus, Thaddaeus, Simon the Zealot and Judas Iscariot, who betrayed him. Mark 3:13-19

Jesus got away from the crowds up on a mountainside 'and called to him those he wanted'. Prior to this event, in the previous chapter, Mark records in verse 15, 'there were many who followed him'. Matthew 10:1-4 and Luke 6:12-16 also record this event and in Luke, the very next verse after this event refers to 'a large crowd of his disciples'. It seems that Jesus already had a fairly large group of followers from which Jesus chose twelve and appointed them to be apostles. The sovereignty of Jesus is emphasised in this story: it is Jesus who called and he appointed those he wanted. Jesus designated the twelve 'apostles', which derives from a Greek verb meaning to send. They were sent to do a special job.

Here Mark lists three things the apostles are to do. They are to be with Jesus, preach and drive out demons. Notice the way it is worded. Their prime purpose is stated in verse 14, 'that they might be with him'. Their primary function is not to preach or cast out demons but to be *with* Jesus, to 'be continually in the company of their Rabbi'.[1] Their relationship with Jesus is to be of first importance; above all else the apostles were to be his friends and companions. Their secondary purposes are to preach and to have the authority to cast out demons.[2] These are the things Jesus was already doing and the apostles are called to join Jesus in his work. It is important to note that it is *being with* Jesus that qualified the disciples to do the work of Jesus. Mark implies that it is only because they are with Jesus that they have authority to preach and cast out demons. Without Jesus they could do none of these things.[3] Jesus establishes here a mentor style of learning. 'These disciples are not rabbinic students, learning the law 'book-ishly', they are to learn by 'walking after Jesus'. They gain their knowledge and sense of mission by being 'with Jesus'.[4]

The rest of the section consists of the names of the apostles. Some of the comments Mark makes about these men give important insights into the way Jesus led and developed his team. These will be explored in due course.

The following aspects of team leadership can be identified in this story.

The primary purpose of the team is to be with Jesus

The disciple's relationship with Jesus was of primary importance, not the work that they did for Jesus. What Jesus wants first is relationships with his people and those relationships should form the basis of whatever else we do. The first responsibility of leaders of ministry teams is to live in a close relationship with Jesus. Their first concern for team members should not be the tasks that those team members perform, but their relationship with Jesus.

Our first priority should be to nurture relationships with Jesus. First we are to be with Jesus, then to preach and serve. The first priority is relationship, then action.

The twelve apostles enjoyed a face to face relationship with Jesus who they could see and touch. Like us, Paul did not have that sort of physical relationship with Jesus yet wrote, ' I want to know Christ'.[5] Today we can still have a relationship with Jesus even though we can't see or touch him physically. I asked a number of Christian leaders how they nurture their relationship with Jesus. They all referred to the importance of Bible reading. All believe that they allow Jesus to speak to them as they read the Scriptures although they select Bible readings in different ways. One leader said that he read through whole Bible books systematically, but another also read specific Bible passages that seem to parallel the situations and issues that he is facing at any time.

Predictably, prayer also figured strongly as a way of nurturing a relationship with Jesus. One person emphasised the need to allow substantial time for prayer, so as to allow time to reflect and allow Jesus to speak during the process of meditation. Another talked about contemplative prayer: times that move between meditation and prayer. That person also followed the discipline of daily and weekly prayer lists. All of these leaders read substantially and testified to the importance of quality Christian literature. Some use published liturgies to stimulate meditation while others find that biographies provide insights into the relationships other people have had with Jesus.

Most said that relationships with other people strongly influence their relationships with Jesus. One referred to helpful mentoring relationships, while another spoke about the perspectives gained through a group of Christian friends. The relationships that are most helpful are with people who will lovingly tell the truth. One leader said that he was greatly helped by spending time with 'broken' people who had suffered greatly, because such people have unique perspectives about knowing Jesus.

Commitment to Jesus is important if we are to have a relationship with him. We need to know the Scriptures and be diligent in applying them to our lives. Jesus said, 'If anyone loves me he will obey my teaching'.[6] One man said that his understanding of what it means to know Jesus keeps growing, so his relationship with Jesus keeps growing.

Other things people found helpful were writing journals and reflecting on Christian music. One person emphasised that his relationship is affected by his overall well-being. He ensures that he gets plenty of sleep. He also takes time to be aware of his emotional state and be honest before God about whether he is feeling anxious, afraid, angry and so on. He believes that being in touch with himself helps him to maintain a close relationship with Jesus.

Assign tasks to the team

One of the main differences between a team and a random crowd is a common purpose. Jesus knew what he wanted his team to do and he clearly identified the tasks he expected them to perform. In Mark's Gospel, two tasks were identified. The first was that the disciples were to preach. The Greek word translated 'preach' means to be a herald.[7] This implied a discipline about what was to be said, because heralds did not deliver their own messages but those of the governments they represented. Christian leaders must be careful to present God's message and not just their own opinions. Preaching is not just religious public speaking. Preachers must study the Word of God so that they will be able to pass on God's message.

The apostles' second task was to drive out demons. There is a great deal of debate about how this applies to people in the twenty-first century and it does not serve the purpose of this book to enter that debate. I can probably embrace the views of most Christians by affirming that one of our tasks is to oppose evil. Christian leadership is to engage evil, whether it is generalised in values, attitudes and actions, institutionalised in unjust social structures or personified in spiritual beings, as it is often the case in the gospel narratives.

Matthew's account of this incident adds 'to heal every disease and sickness'[8] to the list of apostles' responsibilities. Once again, there is considerable contemporary debate about healing, but for the purposes of this book it is enough to affirm that Jesus wants us to be concerned about the physical well-being of people. Mark focused on the spiritual dimensions of leadership responsibilities, preaching and casting out demons. Matthew recorded Jesus' concern that his disciples address physical as well as the spiritual needs. According to Jesus the scope of Christian leadership is holistic. We cannot address spiritual issues like personal salvation and forgiveness and turn our backs on poverty, sickness and injustice. On the other hand we cannot focus on the physical and social needs of human beings and ignore their desperate need for a relationship with God.

These three tasks of preaching, healing and opposing evil reflected the leadership of Jesus. These are the things that Jesus did because he believed in the message of the kingdom, stood opposed to evil and valued the sick and disabled. At this point the apostles were commissioned to take up the work for themselves, so that they would do the same things that Jesus had done. As in all transformational leadership, the disciples joined with Jesus in a mutual purpose. They were no longer just willing to be associated with Jesus, they began to do the things that Jesus was doing: to preach, cast out demons, and heal.

There are three lessons that contemporary leaders can learn from Jesus when assigning tasks to teams.

The tasks should be holistic

Develop a concern for whole people and address both physical and spiritual needs.

The tasks should be mutual

Don't ask people to do what you don't do yourselves. Call them to join you in the work you are already doing.

The tasks should be clear

Be able to clearly describe what teams are expected to do. Teams can't perform well unless they clearly understand the tasks.

Pray for the team

From Luke's account we learn that before Jesus chose his twelve apostles, he spent the whole night in prayer (Luke 6:12-16). Mark 6:46 and Mark 14:32-42 also show that Jesus spent considerable time in prayer prior to making important decisions and before important events. We read that Jesus also specifically prayed for his disciples and the content of one of those prayers is recorded for us in John 17:6-19. Furthermore, Jesus taught his disciples to pray (Matthew 6:5-13). The importance of prayer in Christian leadership needs to be emphasised. We must follow the example of Jesus, who prayed to his Father about his own decisions and responsibilities, prayed for his team and taught his team to pray.

Develop an inner circle

Francis Moloney[9] claimed that it is significant that only three apostles, Peter, James and John, were given special names by Jesus in Mark's account. He believes that Mark recorded these second names to indicate the disciples who were to be drawn into an even closer relationship with Jesus: an inner circle within an inner circle. What would be the purpose of recording their special names, if it were not to signal some special function for these particular men? Whether or not Moloney is correct in his interpretation of this particular text, he is correct in his analysis of the team structure of Jesus' disciples. Jesus had a closer relationship with Peter, James and John, than the other disciples. They were included at times when the other disciples were not. For example, they witnessed the Transfiguration (Mark 9:2), accompanied Jesus during Gethsemane (Mark 14:32), witnessed the resurrection of Jairus' daughter (Luke 8:51) and Peter and John were given responsibility to prepare for the Passover (Luke 22:8).

An inner circle that is held in closer relationship and given greater responsibility is a healthy leadership practice. Unless a group is small, it may not be possible to include everyone within such a close relationship but it is unhealthy to have no one. This was one of the issues that contributed to the failure of Ken's leadership, described in the story that opened this chapter. Ken would not allow an inner circle and as a result, both Ken and his team suffered. He would have been far more effective if he had established an inner circle within the larger team, one in which he could consult, share important information and gain support in dealing with difficult issues. Effective leaders are not lone rangers, riding way out in front of the pack; they share the load with trusted colleagues.

Expect failure

Mark's list of disciples concluded with a reference to the fact that Judas would betray Jesus. Moloney[10] observed that this is the first time in Mark's gospel that reference is made to the possible failure of a disciple. The failure of the disciples becomes a very dominant theme as Mark's gospel progresses. All the disciples failed by the end of Mark, yet Jesus did not fail his failing disciples. We will all encounter failure and the way we respond is crucial.

'We make heaps of mistakes. Lots of things we try seem to fail.' These were the words of a very successful youth worker. Within about three years he had built a small youth group into a large youth program that attracted crowds of young people and achieved lots of worthwhile outcomes. Why then did he talk about failures? If this ministry was so successful, how come they made so many mistakes?

The idea of a competent leader making mistakes should not surprise us. Success is often intertwined with failure. This youth worker had not always stuck with the traditional methods of youth work but had been willing to test new ideas. Some of these failed but his willingness to experiment kept his youth work on the cutting edge. Better ways are often discovered only after other ways have been tried and found inadequate. A healthy attitude to failure, therefore, is a necessary component of success. People will be reluctant to try new ideas if they are afraid of failure, or if they live in a climate of criticism where their mistakes are eagerly thrown back in their faces. On the other hand innovation and creativity blossom amongst people who are not afraid to risk attempting new things.

The fear of failure can dramatically hinder growth and learning. A young man once told me how much he was bored with work because his job involved menial office tasks, yet he was clearly intelligent and capable. When I explored with him the possibility of doing more training and seeking a more interesting position, he explained that he realised that he was capable of this, but in another position he might make mistakes. That was the approach he took to most of life. He rarely tried anything new and life was lived avoiding anything with the possibility of failure. He was bored and unhappy, but at least he did not make mistakes. When the fear of failure dominates, we shrink away from the opportunities for growth and learning.

Failure is inevitable. The important thing is to learn from mistakes. Such learning might not take place however, if we take the attitude that mistakes are not allowed. Warren Bennis[11] emphasised the value of learning from adversity and mistakes. Where mistakes are not allowed, creativity is squashed and valuable lessons are lost as mistakes are either concealed or reinterpreted as success. Patrick Duignan[12] wrote that an insistence on perfection impedes learning because, in environments where only the best is acceptable, faults tend to be denied. Leadership should encourage the risk taking that allows for learning by mistakes. Concealing or denying mistakes or reinterpreting them to make it seem as if nothing went wrong, might help us feel more comfortable but valuable lessons are lost. If we accept mistakes as part of life, we are more likely to examine them. This will result in learning and growth.

None of this means that we should be careless or that we do not have an obligation to avoid mistakes that can be reasonably anticipated. This is particularly important with regard to our duty of care. Leaders cannot afford to take risks with the physical, moral and spiritual safety of the people in our care. It does mean though, that it is unwise to allow the fear of failure to so dominate that we are afraid to experiment with new methods, ideas and models. To shrink from opportunities for fear of making mistakes is a guaranteed way to stifle creativity, innovation and growth.

We need to also be careful how we respond when other people fail, especially the people we lead. They need to develop their abilities and discover their gifts. This requires experimentation and involves a risk of failure. People often discover what they can do by trial and error. If people are not allowed to fail, the discovery and development of their gifts, talents and abilities can be squashed.

Jesus was very tolerant of failure. He maintained relationships with his disciples despite their repeated, serious failures. Jesus encouraged risk taking (for example Mark 8:34-38) and did not shield the disciples from situations where failure was a possibility (for example Mark 6:7-13). When failures occurred he helped his disciples to reflect on their mistakes and used failure as an opportunity for learning (for example Mark 10:13-16,35-45). Jesus was a great example of a leader who responded lovingly and patiently to failure in his followers. The disciples of Jesus failed in a great many ways and Jesus graciously persevered with them. He never gave up on his disciples even when they had all deserted him, one disciple had denied him and a former disciple had even betrayed him. Jesus persevered with failing disciples and helped them to grow through their mistakes. Failure is rarely pleasant or comfortable, but it can be one of the greatest teachers.

Prepare for leadership succession

There are many examples of organisations, movements and ministries that came to an end or were severely set back, when the leader died or moved on. Everything was going fine and moving ahead until the leader left for some reason and there was no one to take his or her place. Everyone was caught up in the activities of the moment without stopping to think about who would carry on the work in the future. I have often been surprised to find people in leadership roles who have given little or no thought to leadership succession. They simply have no answers to questions like, 'Who is likely to be able to replace you when you finish in your leadership role?' Or, 'What is being done to prepare people to take over, when you vacate your current position?' Advertising and hiring suitable people can replace some leaders in professional positions. However in many churches and Christian organisations, a great many of the leadership roles are voluntary and people need to be nurtured and trained to be able to fill leadership positions when the needs arise. I have been delighted to discover leaders who plan for their own replacement. They can name the people who are likely to be the future leaders and can describe how those people are being trained and prepared.

Just as Mark singled out the inner circle of Peter, James and John by giving them special names, Matthew and Luke singled out Peter using the same device (see Matthew 10:2; Luke 6:14). As stated in point 4 above, Francis Moloney[13] claimed that this is how Matthew and Luke identified the person who was to become the leader of the apostles following the death of Jesus. The role of Peter and the other apostles in the early church is a subject of considerable debate. Some believe that Peter was the first pope while, at the other end of the spectrum, there are those who believe that the early church had no leader but Jesus. It is clear that Peter, James, Paul, Apollos and numerous others exercised leadership in the early church. The early Christians had no Saviour and Lord but Jesus, but that does not mean that other Christians were not leaders. Genuine Christian leaders are not rivals to Jesus but they are God's gift to help their fellow Christians to follow Jesus. 'It was he (that is, Jesus) who gave some to be apostles, some to be prophets, some to be evangelists, and some to be pastors and teachers, to prepare God's people for works of service, so that the body of Christ may be built up until we all reach unity in the faith and in the knowledge of the Son of God and become mature, attaining to the whole measure of the fullness of Christ.'[14]

In the early chapters of The Acts of the Apostles, Peter was clearly playing the role of leader of the early church in Jerusalem. He began to play that role within a couple of months of the death and resurrection of Jesus. Obviously a lot of developments took place in Peter's life soon after the death of Jesus, to change him from the disciple that denied Jesus to the preacher who would stand up and address the crowd on the Day of Pentecost (Acts 2). The realisation that Jesus had risen from the dead and the coming of the Holy Spirit were some of the events that transformed Peter. However before Jesus died, he trained Peter and the other disciples for their future leadership roles so that they would be prepared for what lay ahead. Jesus knew he was leaving and prepared Peter and other apostles to lead his followers. Leaders today should follow Jesus' example and plan for their own replacements.

Train the team

I remember well my short time as a Sunday school teacher. When I was 15 years old the director of the Sunday school of my church asked me to become a Sunday school teacher. No training was offered and I was given some lesson material and assigned as the sole teacher to a class of boys who were probably about ten years old. It was a disaster. The boys misbehaved constantly and at the end of each 'lesson' I had little reason to believe that they had learnt much at all. At the time I thought that these were very naughty boys, but later realised that they were just normal children and that the problem was that I did not know how to teach, or manage behaviour and I did not even know a great deal about the Bible. I hated being a Sunday school teacher and I think that the boys in my class also hated it. I endured until the end of that year but then gave up and never taught Sunday school again. I found other avenues of Christian service and it took many years before I regained the confidence to attempt to work with primary aged children again.

The story of the appointing of the apostles in Mark's gospel and the sequence of events that surround it, provide some insights into processes used by Jesus to prepare the disciples for leadership roles. In the first two chapters of Mark, Jesus called his disciples. In chapter three they were appointed as apostles. During the first six chapters of Mark the disciples accompanied Jesus, and learnt from Jesus by watching and listening. In Mark 6:7, Jesus sent the disciples out on mission from which they returned and reported on what they had done (Mark 6:30). Anton Baumohl[15] described the training practices of Jesus in the following way.

> Jesus was not only an outstanding teacher; he was also an accomplished trainer. He trained the disciples in preparation for the various activities in which they were soon to become involved. Jesus' training style involved a form of apprenticeship where the disciples watched as he worked before being sent out to have a go for themselves. Imagine how the disciples felt as they went out on their first solo run (Luke 9:1-6, 10). They had heard the theory and seen it work in practice, they were even aware of some of the potential problems and opposition – and now they were being sent out on their own. Imagine their return. What mixed feelings they would share with Jesus – the exhilaration of having accomplished a worthwhile task, the sense of failure over experiences of rejection or tasks unfinished, the relief at getting back to a secure environment. In today's jargon that important meeting with Jesus recorded in verse 10 would probably be called a 'debrief' or 'supervisory session'!...
>
> ...Three elements can be identified in Jesus' apprenticeship training.
>
> OBSERVATION   EXPLANATION   INVOLVEMENT
>
> This apprenticeship lasted the three years of Jesus' public ministry and then the disciples were, in one respect, on their own – 'articles' completed but still learning and developing as they got on with the task.

Both apprenticeship training and supervision are effective modern training methods and Anton Baumohl[16] explained the difference between them in the following way.

> Apprenticeship involves the person being trained working alongside someone already involved in the work. To begin

with they observe and note what is happening. Then they are allowed to take responsibility for parts of the work – being watched over by the experienced worker. When they are ready they take total responsibility, still watched by the experienced worker. And finally they are let loose on their own. Apprenticeship offers immediate experience of the actual work in its real context...

...Supervision, like apprenticeship, is a form of on-the-job training. It is also ideally suited to the training of individuals and small groups. Unlike apprenticeship it does not involve the trainer in acting as a model or require the trainer's presence at every activity in which the learner is involved. The supervisor's role is more akin to a counsellor than a model – helping people to examine and explore their early experiences on the job and to identify the issues raised, the problems encountered and their own feelings as learners. The supervisor is often more remote from the work situation than the apprenticeship trainer and is able to be more objective when helping the person being trained.

My teenage experience of Sunday school teaching could have been so different. Instead of being given a class of my own, I could have been put with an experienced teacher to learn, like an apprentice, by watching and doing. In that context I could have been given parts of lessons to teach until my skills and knowledge had developed to the point where I was ready to have my own class. If I had been older and more skilled, supervision may have been an adequate training approach.

While Jesus used the active learning methods described above, the gospels also refer to the use of direct instruction by Jesus as a training method. On some occasions Jesus just talked to his disciples and told them what he wanted them to know. One example is in Matthew 10:5-42 where Jesus prepared his disciples to go out on mission. He told them where to go, what to do, what equipment to take, where to stay, how to respond to acceptance and also how to respond to rejection.

Jesus used a variety of training methods to prepare his team.

These included apprenticeship training, direct instruction and other learning processes that have been referred to earlier in this book, like learning from failure and mentoring. No one training method does it all. Different people learn in different ways and different skills are taught using different methods. It should be noted that Jesus took three years to train his team. He did not just run an afternoon training event and then assume that his team was trained because they had attended the event. Jesus knew that it takes time for people to develop the knowledge, skills and attitudes required for Christian ministry.

Finally, it is important to realise that the training of the disciples had a conclusion. The gospels end with Jesus leaving the disciples, at least in a physical sense, so that there is recognition of the conclusion of the training process. Matthew's gospel ends with the disciples being commissioned to go and do the job themselves. 'Go and make disciples of all nations'[17]. Jesus promised that he would still be with them, but it was not like it was before. Their training was now over but this did not mean that their learning was over. The Acts of the Apostles shows that they had to struggle with many new and difficult situations as the gospel spread into other cultures and as the church grew. The disciples had to keep learning for the rest of their lives but they learned as men who were already trained.

Training does not go on forever. There is a difference between training and on-going learning. Learning goes on forever, while training occurs over specific periods to prepare people for particular roles and tasks. Eventually trainees should see themselves as trained and get on with doing the job. It is imperative that trainers also recognise that there should be an end to the training process, so that a different type of relationship can develop with the former trainees. The degree of scrutiny and supervision that is normal during training should not continue unchanged after people are trained. People should still be accountable, but, once trained, they should be held accountable like other trained team members, not like trainees. If the relationship between trainer and trainee is assumed to be a permanent training relationship, the trainee is disempowered and becomes forever subservient to the trainer. The training relationship should be seen as a temporary relationship that empowers and equips, and then sets people free.

Training is a crucial responsibility for leaders and there are many training methods that can be used. The purpose of training is to equip people for roles and responsibilities. Once that has been achieved they should get on with the job, and their training for those tasks should then be recognised as finished.

ENDNOTES

1. Cole, R.A, *The Gospel According to St. Mark. An Introduction and Commentary,* The Tyndale Press, 1961, pp. 79.

2. Cole, R.A, *The Gospel According to St. Mark. An Introduction and Commentary,* The Tyndale Press, 1961, pp. 79.

3. Moloney, Francis J, *Disciples and Prophets,* Great Britain: Darton, Longman and Todd Ltd, 1980, pp.139.

4. Moloney, Francis J, *Disciples and Prophets,* Great Britain: Darton, Longman and Todd Ltd, 1980, pp.139.

5. Philippians 3:10

6. John 14:23

7. Arndt, William F & Gingrich, F. Wilbur, *A Greek-English Lexicon of the New Testament and Other Early Christian Literature,* University of Chicago Press, 1958, pp.431.

8. Matthew 10:1

9. Moloney, Francis J, *Leadership in the Christian Scriptures,* 1996, This view was presented in a series of lectures presented at the Australian Catholic University, Brisbane.

10. Moloney, Francis J, *Disciples and Prophets,* Darton, Longman and Todd Ltd, 1980, pp.139.

11. Bennis, Warren, *On Becoming a Leader,* Addison Wesley Publishing Company, 1989, pp.95-100.

12. Duignan, Patrick A, *The Dance of Leadership: At the Still Point of the Turning World.* Australian Council for Educational Administration, 1997, pp.7-10.

13. Moloney, Francis J, *Leadership in the Christian Scriptures,* 1996, This view was presented in a series of lectures presented at the Australian Catholic University, Brisbane.

14. Ephesians 4:11-13

15. Baumohl, Anton, *Grow Your Own Leaders, A Practical Guide to Training in the Local Church,* Scripture Union, 1987, pp. 20-21.

16. Baumohl, Anton, *Grow Your Own Leaders, A Practical Guide to Training in the Local Church,* London: Scripture Union, 1987, pp. 69 and 80.

17. Matthew 28:19

looking forward

A pastor's struggle

Listen to Barry's thoughts as he wrestles with preparing for the annual Christmas service.

> Another Christmas rolls around and it's a prayerful time as I sit down to write my sixteenth Christmas message. I have never lost the passion for declaring this good news – I just want to make it as fresh as the first day it was delivered. My greatest delight and most humbling responsibility is to preach Christ. I felt the strongest urges to leave school teaching and become a pastor. I believed that God was leading me to teach the scriptures to God's people, and reach out to the lost around us.
>
> Some of those prodigals will be at the Christmas 'service' – I want desperately to connect with this decreasing audience that comes once or twice a year, I want to be clear and honest and for God to challenge them – what songs, items, drama will reach them? And as I prepare I know there will members of the 'club' – with their critical eye, muttering … 'this is NOT how it is done'. I am always faced with those who seek to make ministry and 'church' just a comfortable event. Because of this, I find it a struggle, to do the Lord's work and keep his priorities as my priorities. With the Lord's help, I want to follow a ministry agenda consistent with that of Jesus Christ and Him crucified – and live a genuine life before others. May I never lose the focus and the passion for doing what Jesus wants me to do.

When Barry first decided to become a pastor, he imagined himself doing the things that Jesus did, preaching the gospel, teaching the Bible and caring for people in need. As he looks back on years of ministry, he has found that most of the Christians, who employ him, really want him to pander to the whims of a Christian club. Yet Barry has not given in and is committed to striving to embrace the mission agenda of Jesus, not just play the church game. It's tough going and it would be a lot easier if more Christians were striving with Barry to follow the leadership principles of Jesus.

The leadership of Jesus - principles and practices

This book has considered four gospel stories about Jesus and identified many principles and practices that can be observed in his leadership. As a reminder, it would be helpful to assemble the issues that have been covered. Here is a summary of the main points about leadership that have been identified.

Change-focused leadership
(Chapter 2)

The goal of leadership is change

- The focus is transformation not organisation
- The emphasis is on qualitative change, not quantitative change
- The willingness to change is a prerequisite of leadership
Leaders begin with the end of a change process in mind

Following is essential in the change process

Leadership is about change while management is about production

- Leadership is an influence relationship while management is an authority relationship
- Leadership involves leaders and followers while management involves managers and subordinates
- Leadership intends real change while management produces or sells goods and/or services
- Leadership reflects mutual purposes while management focuses on coordinating activities

It is God who calls people into a change process

The need for change is urgent

People-centred leadership
(Chapter 3)

Christian leadership meets human need

Christian leadership engages human frailty

- Jesus is different and in some ways we cannot be like him
- Christian leadership begins with recognition of our own frailty
- Christian leadership involves helping others recognise their frailty

Different human relationships produce different types of leadership

- Transactional leadership
- Transformational leadership
- Charismatic leadership

To lead means to influence people

People respond to leaders who impart vision

Value-based leadership
(Chapter 4)

Jesus displayed inclusiveness as a key value

Jesus displayed identification as a key value

Christian symbols should connect with the values of Jesus

Some values should have a higher priority

The values of Jesus lead to conflict

Team-empowering leadership
(Chapter 5)

The primary purpose of the team is to be with Jesus

Assign tasks to the team

- The tasks should be holistic
- The tasks should be mutual
- The tasks should be clear

Pray for the team

Develop an inner circle

Expect failure

Prepare for leadership succession

Train the team

To follow the example of Jesus means to strive to embrace these leadership principles. Leadership that results from following Jesus will be change-focussed, people-centered, value-based and team-empowering.

The leadership of Jesus - general observations

How is the leadership of Jesus, as displayed in the gospels, different from, or similar to, the leadership practiced by other leaders? When we step back from all the stories and consider the leadership practices and principles of Jesus, the following general observations can be made.

The leadership of Jesus is unique in some ways

Jesus is the Son of God. He possessed supernatural qualities that allowed him to perform miracles like no other person who has ever lived. This ability to do great things meant that Jesus had a unique capacity to influence people. Apart from his ability, Jesus also had a unique story. He was born of a virgin, having been conceived by the Holy Spirit. When he was baptised, 'a voice from heaven said, 'This is my Son, whom I love; with him I am well pleased' (Matthew 4:17). On one occasion, Jesus was transfigured before some of his disciples. His clothes became dazzling white and Elijah and Moses appeared from centuries past and were talking to Jesus. Knowledge of events like these filled many people with awe. Jesus' supernatural capacity and his unique story meant that he exercised a leadership that was unique in many respects.

The leadership of Jesus is consistent with the leadership of other leaders in many respects

Having acknowledged that the leadership of Jesus is unique in some ways, it is important to recognise also that a lot of his leadership principles and dynamics are present in many other leaders. Much of what we have explored in Chapters 2 to 5 is common leadership practice. Jesus focused on qualitative change, not just maintaining the organisation. He began with the end in mind. Jesus affirmed followers and following. He was a powerful influence and developed a mutual purpose with his followers. Jesus practiced a transformational brand of leadership, and addressed human need with a sense of urgency. He knew how to impart vision in a way that moved people to respond. Jesus had very clear values and ensured that the symbols he used connected with those values. He had a clear hierarchy of values and upholding those values often resulted in conflict. Jesus developed and trained a team. He was clear about the purpose of his team and assigned tasks to them. Jesus developed a structure within his team and prepared for leadership succession. He expected that failure would occur within his team and used failure as an opportunity for teaching.

Much of this could be said about many leaders. These principles of leadership are not unique to Jesus, but they can be found in many contexts where leadership occurs, both Christian and non-Christian. In many ways Jesus went about leadership using a lot of the same principles that are used by other leaders. While Jesus was unique, there are many aspects of his leadership that can, and should, be adopted by Christian leaders today. He is the unique Son of God, but he forever remains our example.

The leadership of Jesus contrasts with much of contemporary Christian leadership

While there are contemporary examples of Christian leadership that do embrace many of the leadership principles and practices of Jesus, there are others that stand in contrast to Jesus. These principles have been explored through Chapters 2 to 5, but allow me to remind you of a sample. Jesus was driven by the need for change, while many Christians are so dominated by tradition that they avoid change at any cost. While Jesus focused on the transformation of lives, many Christians focus their energy primarily on organisational procedures. Jesus focused on qualitative change, yet many seem to ignore how God wants us to change and merely aim to make more people just like us. The disciples were personally called by the Son of God into their ministries and given positions as apostles, yet they clearly made mistakes and were open to reproof. There seems to be an increasing number of pastors and Christian leaders who apparently believe that their position or call makes them almost infallible and above criticism. Jesus practiced transformational leadership, yet today transactional leadership is far more common, even in contexts where transformational leadership is achievable.

Jesus' leadership agenda was based on values, not on political expediency or keeping the members happy. His hierarchy of values put mission and compassion ahead of tradition and comfort, in stark contrast to typical, western churches of today. If his values led to conflict, Jesus did not back away as if the popularity of his religious 'product' was his chief concern. One of Jesus' chief values was inclusiveness in contrast to strategies of exclusiveness often promoted in the contemporary scene. Jesus also gave identification a high value, yet many contemporary leaders remain aloof from ordinary people. I could go on with example after example. Suffice to say that there are many ways in which the leadership of Jesus contrasts with the leadership of many Christian leaders today.

These aspects of leadership that contrast with Jesus are not just lapses but practices that are often embraced quite intentionally. Many of these areas of contrast involve a failure to truly embrace the mission, values and beliefs of Jesus. Compassion, mission, grace, sacrifice and humility are cast aside in favour of maintaining tradition, entertaining the Christian club or competing with other Christian groups for market share, both human and financial. It is a great irony that Christian leaders, who see their role as leading others in following Jesus, fail so miserably themselves to follow Jesus, even in the exercise of their Christian leadership role.

Recommendations

There have been many challenges and suggestions made during the course of this book, but at this point I would like to make thirteen recommendations.

1. Christian leadership practices should be critiqued. They should be critiqued against the Bible and more specifically, against the example of Jesus. More important than political expediency, convenience or making people happy, we should think a great deal about how our practices fit with those of Jesus.

2. We should recognise that there is a difference between leadership and management. Both functions are important, but they are not the same. If management is neglected, ministry is disorganised. If leadership is neglected, we will fail to affirm the values of Jesus and we will avoid the struggle for the changes that Jesus seeks.

3. While we may sometimes have to settle for transactional leadership, we should strive for transformational leadership.

4. We should aim to be Christ-like, serving others and addressing human need, rather than focusing on organisational growth.

5. While Christians should respect their leaders, every leader should be accountable. Claims by pastors and Christian leaders that their position (or their call by God) puts them above criticism should be vigorously rejected.

6. We should evaluate our hierarchy of values. The values that are most important should be given the highest priority and the greatest weight in determining ministry direction.

7. We should give priority to qualitative goals over quantitative goals. Real change means changes in beliefs, values and actions, not just numbers.

8. We should affirm the importance of followers in the leadership process.

9. We should affirm the values of Jesus, like identification and inclusiveness. That means rejecting ministry practices that pander to pride and promote exclusiveness.

10. We should expect conflict to result from affirming the values of Jesus, but our response should be Christ-like.

11. We should expect failure but embrace it as the opportunity to learn.

12. We should affirm the importance of our relationship with God, fervently pursue God, and encourage all team members to do the same.

13. We should aim to influence people rather than coerce them. People only really change when they have chosen to do so freely.

The ongoing call to follow Jesus

For some Christians, leadership itself has become a false god. The status of leadership and the power that often comes with leadership positions can be highly treasured. Some seek leadership, not as a means to a ministry end, but as an end in itself. When the lust for leadership takes hold, people go to great lengths to 'gain power', even if they are unsure of their own direction. When this mindset prevails, the way of Jesus can be easily cast aside. Is it really all that important to be a leader? I know it is vitally important for the followers of Jesus to have effective contemporary leaders. But does it have to be *you* that becomes the leader? Does it have to be *me*? Did Jesus command us all to be leaders?

Did Jesus command any of us to be leaders?

When Jesus was calling his disciples he was recruiting those who would become leaders of the early church. In Chapter 2, I pointed out that Jesus did not command them to lead, but to follow. At the risk of repeating myself, I would like to conclude this book with an appeal for Christian leaders to *always* see themselves primarily as followers. Jesus met disciple after disciple with the command to 'follow me' (Matthew 4:19; 9:9; Mark 1:17; 2:14; Luke 5:27; John 1:43). Even though Jesus was obviously developing leaders, he expressed more concern that his disciples be followers. On some occasions when the disciples seemed to express leadership ambition, Jesus was not impressed (See Mark 9:33-37; 10:35-45).

We should not be too ambitious to be leaders. We are not all commanded to lead. We are all commanded to follow: to follow Jesus. If, in the course of following Jesus, others follow us, then we emerge as Christian leaders. But if that does not happen, it does not really matter, because our primary call is not to lead but to *follow* Jesus.

People become leaders when other people follow them, so without followers, leaders cannot exist. Only a minority of people can be the leaders at any one time. The vast majority must be followers. It was like this in the early church where the majority of Christians were followers who worked with a minority of leaders, like Peter and Paul. Without followers, leaders can achieve very little. To think of leadership as only the activity of leaders is to disregard some of the most important dynamics in the whole process. Leadership is not about special people with special abilities who do it all for everybody else. Leadership is about a relationship between leaders and followers in which the leaders and followers work together to achieve their goals. Let us endorse following and be prepared to be followers ourselves.

Let us commit ourselves to follow Jesus. Whether or not we see ourselves as leaders, let us follow him. If we are leaders, let us follow him in the way we conduct our leadership. Let us aim to embrace the values, principles and practices that were hallmarks of the leadership of Jesus. Let us lead others in following Jesus.

One day, the time will probably come when we will cease to be leaders. When that day comes, let us still follow Jesus. It is far more important to follow Jesus than to lead people. We are not all called to lead. We are all called to follow Jesus.

'Come, follow me,' Jesus said, 'and I will make you fishers of men.' At once they left their nets and followed him.[1]

ENDNOTES

1. Mark 1:17-18

To order titles in the Perspectives
series and other Scripture Union
resources go to:

www.scriptureunion.org.au
www.scriptureunion.org.uk
www.scriptureunion.org.nz

Other Titles in the
Perspectives series...

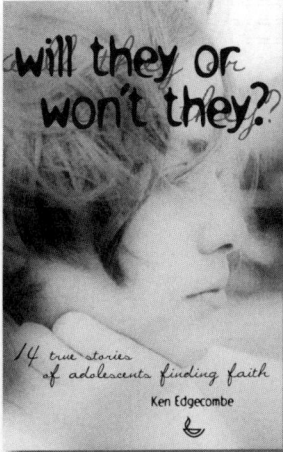

Will they or
Won't they?

Ken Edgecombe

Children and
the gospel

Ron Buckland

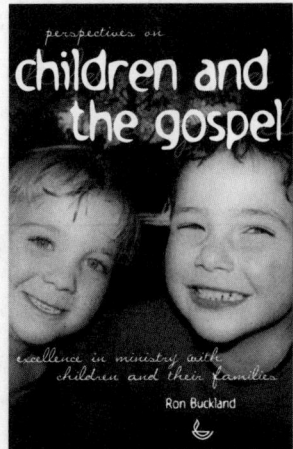